Your Family in Focus

Appreciating
What You Have
Making It
Even Better

Your Family in Focus

Mitch Finley

AVE MARIA PRESS   Notre Dame, Indiana 46556

International Standard Book Number: 0-87793-493-2

Library of Congress Catalog Card Number: 92-75250

Cover photograph by Don Franklin

Cover design by Katherine Robinson Coleman

Printed and bound in the United States of America

Dedication

For my family—my wife, Kathy,
and our three sons,
Sean, Patrick, and Kevin:
You are God's greatest gift to me.

CONTENTS

Introduction

I DON'T KNOW ABOUT YOU, gentle reader, but I dream of an idyllic family life. I would dearly love my family to be free of conflict, free of trouble. I would like us to have smooth sailing all the time. But it doesn't work that way. Something about family life, no matter what form it takes, is decidedly messy and frequently troublesome.

Gilbert Keith Chesterton (1874-1936), probably the most quotable English-speaking Catholic of the twentieth century, hit the nail smack on the head. He said:

> Of course the family is a good institution because it is uncongenial. It is wholesome precisely because it contains so many divergences and varieties. It is . . . like a little kingdom, and, like most other little kingdoms, is generally in a state of something resembling anarchy. . . . Aunt Elizabeth is unreasonable, like mankind. Papa is excitable, like mankind. Our youngest brother is mischievous, like mankind. Grandpapa is stupid, like the world; he is old, like the world.

Chesterton was right. Family life "is wholesome precisely because it contains so many divergences and varieties." If family life was simple, a snap, no trouble at all, it would also be a crashing bore.

We humans crave a challenge. In our heart of hearts we like nothing more than adventure. And family life is challenge upon challenge, one adventure after another.

Of course, since we humans are also sissies and

11

whiners, we tend to complain a lot about the challenges and adventures that can be traced directly to belonging to a family. Ah, but take away that family and we want it back again as soon as possible. Why?

From a Christian point of view, the reason is that family life is the best blend available of divine and human love. It is in our knockabout, laughing and crying life together as family that we touch the depths and reach the heights. It is in our life together as a family that we discover both God and ourselves.

Before I go any further, however, I want to say there is no such thing as "the family." Families come in various sizes, shapes, and descriptions. There are families with and without children, single- and two-parent families, young couples who have no children, older couples whose children are grown and gone, and blended families— families made up of parts of other families divided by divorce or death. Single people continue to belong to the family they grew up in, and widowed people are not without a family. Whatever your family looks like, it is a genuine family.

In this enrichment guide for Catholic families I will talk about some ways family life takes shape among Catholics today. I will also discuss ways families can enrich and nourish their life together. Above all, however, my hope for this book is that it will give you and your family some ideas to talk about that will help your unique family to become even more of a community of love than it already is.

FAMILY FOCAL POINTS

Following each chapter, you will find one or two "Family Focal Points." Each of these is designed to highlight aspects of that chapter. Individuals can use these for reflection. Groups can use them as discussion starters.

Finally, this: No matter what shape your family takes,

remember that it is in your family that you can find what your heart desires more than anything else in the world: love—the love of other people and God's love, too. So cherish your family and prefer it above other treasures. Nothing can take its place.

CHAPTER 1

Hooray for Family Life, Warts and All!

THE PRESIDENT OF THE GROUP introduced me, I rose from my seat and turned to face the audience of some sixty men and women. "Family life," I said, "is holy." Instantly, from the middle of the room, a man called out, "Ha!" Which, naturally, drew much laughter from the entire group.

My critic was only being honest, and most of us, if we are honest, would have to agree with him. "Holy" is not the first word that pops to mind for most of us when we think of family life.

The term holy has an unreal sound; it smacks of a spiritual and moral perfection associated with plaster saints or nature untouched by human hands. We can call a brilliant sunset or a majestic eagle perched atop a tall pine tree holy. But a little knot of people who live together, are related to one another, and squabble over trivialities like who's going to take out the garbage or what to watch on television? Fat chance.

We label Mother Teresa holy because she cares for people she finds dying in the streets of Calcutta. But to call the typical family holy sounds weird. After all, in a family there's a ten-year-old who last year hit his younger brother over the head with a baseball bat so he had to have seven stitches; a younger brother whose sole ambition in life seems to be to one day own an electric bass guitar; a girl who collects postage stamps and hangs posters of rock stars on her bedroom walls; a predictable husband and father who commutes forty-five minutes to and from work every weekday and whose idea of a truly good time is watching the Super Bowl on TV; and a tired wife and mother who doesn't care what the kitchen looks like as long as she can spend a half-hour in her flower garden each summer morning before she leaves for work.

This is holy? Gimme a break!

It all depends, of course, on what we mean by holy. When the Bible says holy, it means whole. The word comes from a Hebrew word that means "separate" or "different." In a culture where conforming and going-along often lead to unhealthy life choices, holy ends up meaning a way of life that is healthy and whole. The English phrase, "hale and hearty," most closely sums up the real meaning of holy.

To be holy is to rejoice in oneself and in the gift of life. That which is holy is healthy, balanced, whole, and charged with enthusiasm for life. Holiness includes such concepts as humor and laughter, compassion and understanding, and the capacity to forgive and be forgiven, to love and be loved. That's what holiness is about.

The point, then, is not that a particular single-parent or traditional two-parent family is automatically a gathering of morally superior individuals or saints. The point is that family life, as a way of living, is a holy way to go. To belong to a family is holy; to commit oneself to marriage is holy; to "fight the unbeatable foe" as a single parent is holy; to live together with these ne'er-do-wells I call my family is, plain and simple, holy. To struggle to be a family is a holy struggle, no matter how far short we may fall of our ideals.

Trying to attain perfection is not what makes family life sacred. What makes it sacred is the fact that to live with people is to live with God. You know that bleary-eyed wonder at the breakfast table with you each morning?

Well, surprise, surprise, that person is as close as you'll ever get to God this side of the grave.

What makes a family holy is not to be totally free from conflict or to become a group of people who never hurt one another. Rather, holiness in families comes from learning to forgive and be reconciled and learning to face up to our problems and do something about them.

I know a family that had to cope with an unwed pregnancy, and I would not hesitate to call this family holy. I know a family that discovered their teen-age daughter was taking the pill and was sexually active. This is a holy family, too. Holy families struggle with alcoholism, and holy families include teen-agers who get involved with drugs. And there are endless holy families that have suffered the effects of painful divorces.

In a holy family, people are frequently unkind to one another, but they keep on trying. Preparing meals, helping a teen-ager learn to drive, listening to one another, changing diapers, cleaning the house, tolerating chaos, and walking up and down with a fussy baby—all this is holy ground.

Family life presents a set of ideals for living together in love, compassion, forgiveness, humor and the hurly-burly of everyday life. To embrace these ideals and strive to live them is a holy project. A family embodies the holiness of family life by striving to be hale and hearty.

Two modern American storytellers give us excellent examples of the kind of family holiness I'm talking about. The first is the great novel by John Steinbeck, *The Grapes of Wrath* (1939). Steinbeck tells the tale of the Joad family, who leave their dust-bitten farm in Oklahoma in the early 1930s. In a broken-down old auto they make the dangerous trek to California in search of a better life.

The strongest character in Steinbeck's story is Ma Joad, who holds the family's world together when it seems most likely to fall apart. "All we got," Ma Joad says, "is the family unbroke. Like a bunch a cows, when the lobos is ranging, stick all together. I ain't scared while we're all here, all that's alive, but I ain't gonna see us bust up."

Through a series of tragedies the Joad family prevails. Grandpa and Grandma Joad die along the way; a good-hearted but simple-minded brother decides to strike off on his own so as not to slow the family down; a young husband abandons Rose of Sharon, the oldest Joad daughter who's expecting a baby; but the family endures, even through violence and injustice.

The Grapes of Wrath is a story of a family holiness that triumphs under the most extreme conditions: uprooted-ness, lack of money and food, unemployment, and back-breaking labor that pays slave wages. No matter how tough things become, Ma Joad reminds the family that while they have one another they have everything: "I ain't scared while we're all here. . ."

Next, in *Breathing Lessons* (1988), Anne Tyler tells the story of Maggie and Ira Moran, an ordinary couple who have been married for twenty-eight years. Tyler reveals a great deal about marriage, its hopes and fears, disappoint-ments, the way children can create storms in a family, and the way husband and wife can fall in love all over again.

Maggie is a scatterbrained, kindhearted dreamer who thinks everything that has gone wrong with other people's lives can be fixed, and she keeps on trying, even though she fails again and again. Ira is quiet, patient, and sensible, but he gave up the career he wanted in medicine in order to support his aging parents, and now he wonders where his life has gone.

Ira and Maggie have two children, now grown: a son who dropped out of high school, can't hold a job, and still thinks he can become a rock star; and a perfectionist daughter who is on her way to the college education her parents never got.

Late in the story, when the weight of the world seems

to be on Maggie's and Ira's shoulders, grace slips in unannounced:

> [Ira] was just as sad as Maggie was, and for just the same reasons. He was lonely and tired and lacking in hope and his son had not turned out well and his daughter didn't think much of him, and he still couldn't figure out where he had gone wrong.
>
> He let his head fall against [Maggie's] shoulder. His hair was thick and rough, strung through with threads of gray that she had never noticed before, that pierced her heart in a way that her own few gray hairs never had. She hugged him tightly and nuzzled her face against his cheekbone. She said, "It will be all right. It will be all right."
>
> And it was, eventually. Don't ask her why.

In spite of their many disappointments, Maggie and Ira show us the grace of ordinary holiness, and they reveal how important friendship is in marriage. Anne Tyler shows us that unlike so many people whose goal in life is to win, Maggie and Ira are here mostly to celebrate. And we would be well-advised to follow their example.

Stories like these help us to be more patient with our own families, and recognize that sometimes the most difficult moments are among the holiest. Such tales help us appreciate the worthwhileness of family life, even in the midst of trials and tribulations. Whether things are going swimmingly, or life seems dark and dreary, the decision we made to dedicate ourselves to marriage and family life is a good one, one worth living and dying for.

In the words of an eighty-five-year-old grandmother, "I never did much that the world calls great. But by damn, my husband and I loved each other for forty-two years, even through the Great Depression, and we stuck by our kids even when they were in trouble. And I'm proud of that. That's something I can carry to the gates of heaven and be proud of."

Of course, it's easier to talk about this than to do it. I

once asked a group of average Catholic parents what they felt most badly about with regard to their own families, and the first thing all of them mentioned was the amount of fighting that went on among family members. Conflict, they said, was unpleasant, and they would love to know how to have less of it. They also said that the less conflict in a family the happier everyone in the family would be and, therefore, the holier that family would be.

I replied that I knew very well from my own family what they were talking about. But this side of never-never land, a conflict-free family life is not only highly unlikely but even undesirable. Family holiness, I said, has more to do with how a family copes with conflict than with how much or how little conflict goes on.

The fact is that family conflict offers great potential for family members to grow in love, wisdom, and a healthy sense of self. In bumping up against one another's rough edges, those edges are slowly worn smooth. Remember, fighting implies love and concern. People who don't love and care for one another don't bother to fight. We don't fight with people we don't love; we ignore them.

I am not, obviously, talking here about destructive forms of family conflict, such as spouse battering or child abuse, whether of a physical or psychological nature. Such abuse is harmful and just plain wrong, and the best move for a family with such problems is to seek immediate professional help.

The fact is that holy, hale and hearty families experience a lot of conflict. They fight fairly, unfairly, constructively and destructively. Sometimes fights have good outcomes, sometimes they don't. Sometimes fights end in smiles, sometimes they just go underground until the next time.

All the same, family members tend to worry about the fact that they seem to fight so much. Be assured, however, that family conflict is normal, and in most cases it does not mean that our families are not hale and hearty. It simply means that all of us are human beings who are still on the way to the Promised Land.

In Chapter 6, which deals with parenting, we will talk in more detail about some of the practical skills families can use to see that conflict remains within the realm of the normal. For now, the important thing to remember is that no family is perfect in the sense of being conflict-free. Healthy, holy families fight a lot, but they also show their love for one another at every opportunity. When we roll all this conflict and love into a ball and toss it into the air, it's called being a family we can be proud of.

FAMILY FOCAL POINT

Dr. Jeffrey Rubin and Dr. Carol Rubin, in their book *When Families Fight*, show that family conflict has been around since the beginning of the human race. Take Adam and Eve:

"For goodness sake, Adam, will you cover up? Get something on now, before somebody comes by and sees you like that!"

"Listen, Eve, I don't know what you're carrying on about. Those fig leaves seem to suggest more than they hide, my dear. So don't you talk. What kind of woman are you, anyhow? Talking to animals. . ."

"It wasn't my idea to come to Paradise. Anyhow, I thought it was your snake."

The point is, of course, that anytime two or more human beings land in the same place at the same time, there is potential for conflict, so we might as well learn to live with it, especially in families.

CHAPTER 2

What's Happening to Family Life Today?

FOR FAMILY LIFE TODAY IT IS the best of times and the worst of times. Families experience stress on several fronts. Most struggle with great courage and fortitude to stay faithful to one another, but many reach the breaking point and snap. Many, especially families headed by single women, have more than their share of challenges to begin with. Still, there is more good news than bad news.

Often, we hear that marriages in the United States end in divorce at an alarming rate, something like 50 percent. Some experts say that our country has the highest divorce rate in the world. Katie, bar the door!

The reality of this depends on how the experts use their numbers. Pollster Louis Harris reported in 1987 that a 50 percent divorce rate is flapdoodle. He said that it isn't fair to take the fact that there are 2.2 million new marriages each year and 1.1 million divorces, and jump to the conclusion that half of all marriages are breaking up.

In reality, all that tells us is that for every two new marriages entered into in a year, an existing one breaks up. Look here says Harris, pocket calculator in hand. There are 57.6 million existing marriages today, right? Right. Of those, only about one million end up in divorce court each year, right? Right. That's not a 50 percent annual divorce rate!

Louis Harris calls to the platform another expert,

Kathryn London, who counts people for the National Center for Health Statistics. She takes a bow and announces that in 1984 only 2.15 percent of existing marriages ended in divorce. Not only that, she adds with a flourish, but that rate has remained almost the same for about the last ten years. So what's all this nonsense about half of all marriages ending in divorce?

It is true, Louis Harris admits, that if *past* trends continue, half of all recent marriages eventually will end in divorce. But he doesn't believe for a moment that this will happen. It's a simple fact, he declares, that such a trend does not exist today. There is much hope for marriage! And the crowd goes wild.

Thank you, thank you, says Harris. He then explains that as far as he is concerned, the mistaken but popular idea that there is a 50 percent *current* divorce rate does nobody any good at all. "How many young people," he asks, "thinking of marriage, tend to have it planted in their heads that their marriage will likely break up?"

It's important to realize that there are definite signs of hope.

First, statistics indicate that people are marrying at a later age. In the mid 1950s, the average age at marriage for men was twenty-two, for women twenty. The statistics for the late 1980s indicate that the average man now waits until about age twenty-four, the average woman until about age twenty-two.

This tendency to postpone saying "I do" may well lead to lasting marriages. The point is not that marrying at a later age will automatically lead to stronger marriages. Rather, waiting allows more time to become the kind of person who can successfully marry.

More young people today decide to get a better education before marrying and to live a little. As a result, they do some growing up before they settle down. Many also want to get a career established and live on their own for some time, rather than move directly from their parents' home into a marriage and family of their own. Perhaps more young people today realize that to walk the highways and byways of life for a while can help them to make a more mature marriage decision later on.

We can see another sign of hope in the development in recent years of marriage preparation policies in many parts of the church in North America. Most dioceses require parishes to provide engaged couples with a formal marriage preparation process that helps them to get ready for marriage in ways they might otherwise overlook.

Usually, this marriage preparation process lasts from three to six months and includes a series of meetings with a priest or deacon who helps the couple talk about their future together in ways they might otherwise overlook.

Sometimes engaged couples also have an opportunity to attend a series of dialogue sessions with an experienced married couple. One version of this is called the Sponsor Couple program. Often, too, future spouses have an opportunity to attend a weekend experience designed especially for them, a church-sponsored program for engaged couples that gives them an opportunity to hear from veteran married couples and discuss with other engaged couples the commitment they are about to make.

Regardless of what a particular marriage preparation process looks like, the point is the church today encourages engaged couples to spend more time getting ready for marriage than they spend getting ready for the wedding.

A third sign of hope comes from couples who take their faith seriously. Several academic studies over the last twenty years indicate that couples who share a strong religious faith have a much lower divorce rate than people who don't. A study done in the mid 1980s concluded that divorce and separation rates for white males is twice as high among those with "no religious preference." This, of course, is simply a negative way of saying something positive: that among those with a "religious preference" the marital success rate is twice as high.

Now that I have raised the important topic of divorce, let's spend some time talking about this from a Catholic perspective.

Divorce is not a matter of two people who are moral failures. Often, in fact, much of the blame for divorce must be placed on causes outside the marriage itself. Frequently, a divorce is at least as much the fault of powerful social and economic forces or an unhealthy family background as it is the fault of the persons involved.

There is no room for couples who are still married to act superior. For example, the more a couple is afflicted by unemployment, irregular employment, low income, or a low level of education, the more likely it is that their marriage will not last.

This places a good deal of responsibility on government and business leaders to do all they can to encourage a society and an economy that is fair to all. If our major concern is the health of marriages and families, for example, there is no such thing as an acceptable level of unemployment, and there should be no tolerance for economic policies that leave families homeless.

Divorce is, of course, a reality. But painful as it is, divorce should never be a cause for despair. Often, people grow and mature a good deal after a failed marriage and later enter a second marriage that is healthy and lasting.

For Catholics, who experience divorce today about as often as do non-Catholics, divorce can be an especially painful experience. Because the church has taken marriage so seriously for so long—and rightly so—divorced Catholics sometimes experience painful guilt that may not be entirely appropriate. Today, Catholics try to uphold the sacred character and integrity of marriage and at the same time express the understanding, compassion, and forgiveness of Christ for those whose marriages fail.

Divorce, in and of itself, does not alienate a person from the church community. Divorce alone does *not* mean that one may no longer receive the sacraments. On the contrary. The church encourages divorced Catholics to continue to turn to the sacraments, especially the eucharist and reconciliation, at every opportunity. These sacraments carry the healing and peace of Christ in a unique way.

Special decisions about their relationship with the church are necessary for divorced Catholics only when they begin to think of remarriage. Even then, however, the church offers the opportunity to remain in full communion with the Catholic community.

The church offers a special process of healing and renewal to divorced persons, whether they are thinking of remarriage or not. The goal of this process is annulment, a formal church declaration which says that the marriage never measured up to the church's standards of a sacramental marriage.

For example, cause for annulment may be found in a lack of maturity on the part of one or both partners when they married, or the presence of an illness such as alcoholism that was not recognized at the time. Either of these could mean that one or both partners were actually unable to live a sacramental marriage.

No divorced and/or remarried Catholic should overlook the possibility of obtaining an annulment. It is possible, even highly likely, that a second marriage can be blessed by the church, even if it did not begin with a church wedding. Even in cases where an annulment is not possible, Catholics should not be without hope.

It is the rare failed marriage today that does not qualify for a church annulment. In such a case, however, a priest, usually in the context of the sacrament of reconciliation, may advise a remarried Catholic who wishes to receive the sacraments to make what is called an *internal forum decision*.

This simply means that in such a situation a remarried Catholic may sincerely believe that he or she has done everything possible to be reconciled with the church. So, that person may prayerfully decide that a loving and forgiving God would want him or her to begin receiving the sacraments again. This *internal forum solution* allows the divorced person who has remarried but whose marriage cannot be blessed by the church, to return to the sacraments in good conscience.

When it comes to divorce and remarriage, we, the church, want to encourage hope, healing, and peace. At the same time, we want to take marriage seriously. The church wants to maintain the ideal of healthy sacramental marriages that last "as long as we both shall live."

Now let's return to our discussion of the status of family life in general today. If we pay attention to little more than the quick newspaper or TV news summaries of various statistics on marriage and family life, it's easy to see a bleak picture. The truth is, however, that most people are happy with their marriages and families.

Louis Harris steps to the podium once again and declares that according to his 1987 poll, eight out of ten families are satisfied—thank you very much—with elements of family life such as relationships among family members, how they cope with money matters, and the balance between work and leisure time.

Harris insists that there is an overwhelmingly positive feeling among people in the United States about the importance of being married and having a family. Ninety-one percent say they would miss family life if they didn't have it.

Often when we ponder the findings of experts who study marriages and families, the conclusions seem to be a mix of good news and bad news, and it can be difficult to "accentuate the positive." But that's what we need to do. Without overlooking the various challenges to family life today, we need to remember that it has a way of renewing itself and bouncing back stronger than ever. The fact is that many positive efforts are being made today to help marriages and families remain strong and healthy.

Marriage Encounter is a good example. Each year two Marriage Encounter organizations, National and Worldwide, lead thousands of basically healthy but, perhaps, blah marriages through a weekend experience that brings new vigor and new life to their relationships. Although Marriage Encounter originated in the Catholic community, now there are Episcopalian, Lutheran, and Jewish Marriage Encounter groups.

Here's another positive fact: Many couples no longer view with alarm the idea of consulting a marriage counselor. Today, when two people find that they are having difficulty dealing with some issue in their marriage, they are about as likely to see a marriage counselor as they are to take their car to a mechanic for a tune-up when it needs it. Nothing could be healthier for marriages than such an attitude.

Finally, an historical perspective can be helpful. Society's attitudes toward marriage and family life have changed a good deal in the last twenty years or so. How do such changes affect real marriages and families?

Although things were different for African-American families and immigrant families, in the 1950s and well into the 1960s, the typical marriage in the United States looked something like the '50s television sitcom, *Ozzie and Harriet.* The family included a husband and father who worked full-time outside the home as the breadwinner and a wife and mother who was a full-time homemaker and parent. It was not unusual for a family to include three, four or more children, and among Catholic families the ideal was even more.

Many families did not fit perfectly into this mold, but

it was the popular family ideal. The family in which I grew up, for example, was smaller than most with only myself and my sister. Mom did not, however, work outside the home. That was unthinkable!

Today, only about 10 percent of all families in the United States fit this traditional image.

Bob and Juanita, an Anglo/Hispanic couple, are more typical of today's married couples. The parents of two children, they both work outside the home. Their oldest child, a girl, goes to school, and the youngest, a boy, spends each weekday in the care of an older woman Bob and Juanita pay to be with their children while they are at work.

It's a struggle to make ends meet, however, and Bob and Juanita worry about what they will do when both children are in school. When that time comes, should they allow their children to be alone in the afternoons until mom and dad get home from work?

Many children today belong to the "latchkey kids" generation, and this is a concern for all of society, not just for the church. Bob and Juanita know that many parents find this necessary, but they don't like the idea. They sometimes argue about the fact that even though Juanita, like Bob, has a full-time job outside the home, she also bears most of the responsibility for keeping the house clean, preparing meals, and meeting the children's needs. Is this fair? Old habits are hard to change, and both she and Bob are reluctant to break out of their established routines.

While it's true that Bob and Juanita struggle with concerns that are common today, they also enjoy advantages that their parents' generation never had. Because Bob and Juanita have a smaller family, they are able to give more of their time and money to each of their children, and they hope that their son and daughter will be able to attend college.

This couple can look forward, also, to at least twenty years together after their children are grown and gone. Active in their parish, Bob and Juanita plan during those years to enjoy life as a couple and, later, their retirement. They also dream about one day joining a lay missionary organization, either in the United States or in another part of the world.

Women in the United States today often find themselves with difficult questions to answer. Mary Ann, a young wife and mother in her mid thirties, works full-time outside the home as a secretary in an insurance agency. Her husband, Leo, is a bank executive. Mary Ann, like Juanita, wonders if it's possible to work as she does and still be a good mother. What's more important she asks: Working to help boost the family income so they can own their home? Or, not working and renting so she can give the children the kind of attention that comes with staying home?

Leo, for his part, puzzles over the amount of time he must be away from his family. He would like to spend more time with his children and wonders if there might be some way he and Mary Ann could each work half-time and stay home half-time.

The problems facing families today are wide-ranging. For example, currently, about 15 percent of all families are headed by single parents and we can expect an increasing number of children to spend at least some of their growing-up years in a family headed by a single parent, usually a mother.

And out-of-wedlock births among teen-agers have reached crisis proportions, a problem that won't be solved by throwing contraceptives at it. Poverty, ignorance, lack of love, simple human frailty, and inadequate family life are as much at fault as is a lack of knowledge of contraceptives or loose morals.

None of these problems are limited to one economic or social class.

What can we do about the many stresses and crises that affect family life today? It seems clear that there should be more governmental support to help families leave poverty behind. Working parents need to be able to find affordable childcare, and parents who choose to stay home to care for children should be rewarded, not penalized, for doing so.

At the same time, married couples can ask themselves if they have their priorities in order from a Christian perspective. Which is more important, striving to maintain an affluent family lifestyle, or making sure we have plenty of opportunity to give needed time and attention to our children and spouses?

What can families do to help themselves, and what can we, the church, offer to help families cope with the challenges of modern life? Perhaps a great part of the answer lies in the fact that Christian families of all kinds are meant to be the most basic form of Christian community, even more basic than the parish. In Chapter 3, I'll tell you the story behind this idea.

FAMILY FOCAL POINT

Scads of young couples these days think it's no big deal to live together. How many of these couples do so because they fear marriage? After all, they have heard that half of all marriages end in divorce!

Of course, we must not neglect the fact that most couples who live together eventually do get married. Most such arrangements last for no more than two or three years, so, undesirable as it is, it's not as if living together is about to replace marriage.

Still, it is glum news that between 1960 and 1987 the number of unmarried couples living together increased from 439,000 to over 2.3 million, and the percentage of unmarried couples raising children increased from 21 percent of this 2.3 million in 1977 to 31 percent in 1987.

Maybe as a nation we would be less frightened of marriage if we listened less to nay-sayers and listened more to time-honored religious and moral traditions as well as our own hearts.

The traditional practice of living separately prior to marriage, and the accompanying tradition of delaying sexual intercourse until marriage, have existed for many, many centuries. These traditions reflect the deep human insight that future spouses need time prior to marriage to get to know one another in ways that living together makes difficult.

Before marriage (and sometimes even after marriage) sexual intimacy can short-circuit growth in a couple's relationship in such areas as communication and practical communication skills. It's easier to "have sex" than to talk about our attitudes toward children, money, or religion.

Sometimes, couples decide to live together before marriage because they think this will be an excellent way to prepare for married life. Several recent studies suggest, however, that this is not likely. These studies reveal that couples who live together before marriage do not have a higher marital success rate than couples who did not live together. If anything, living together before marriage may reveal a basic lack of trust on the part of one or both future spouses that will be a big problem after the wedding.

Donald Joy, author of several books on the role of sexuality in human relationships, argues convincingly that divorce is related more to the pressure to be sexually active before marriage than to any other single cause. On the other hand, when sexual intimacy is reserved for one exclusive relationship, it becomes a powerful force to help spouses remain together through thick and thin.

What about the notion of living together as a trial marriage? The simple truth is that living together is not marriage. Marriage is marriage.

A wedding is not a mere formality. When a couple vows before God and family and friends to remain faithful in good times and bad, no matter what, that makes a profound difference in their relationship. Marriage and living together are similar only in the most superficial ways.

CHAPTER 3

Family Life Is Basic to Church Life

QUICK NOW, WHAT'S THE MOST basic religious activity in which a Catholic family can participate? Did you say, "Going to mass?" In one sense, you're right, but in another important sense you missed by a country mile.

Family life is holy, and to live together loving and serving one another is the most basic religious activity in which any family can engage. When someone asked Jesus what the greatest commandment was, he didn't say: "Go to mass on Sunday," or "Say your prayers every day." Rather, he said that the greatest commandment is to love God with our whole heart, mind, and soul, and our neighbor as ourself.

This is not to say that the eucharist and daily prayer are not important. The point is that going to mass doesn't make sense apart from loving God and other people in everyday life.

As far as Jesus was concerned, faith is a daily affair that should influence our most ordinary occupations and involvements. And because our relationship with God can't be separated from our relationships with other people, the place we encounter God most often is in the people with whom we live most closely on a day in, day out basis.

Indeed, according to an ancient Christian tradition, the family, not the parish, is the most basic form of Christian community.

The late Father Anthony De Mello, S.J., a popular author and spiritual guide, tells a story. There was once a husband and father who went to church each day to perform his religious duties. As the man left his home, he would stop in the doorway, turn and say, "Goodbye, Lord God!" He wisely understood that he met his God most often and most intimately in the hurly-burly of family life.

The tradition that family life is church life goes back to the church's roots in Judaism. To this day, Jewish communities view the family as the fundamental religious unit. The most important celebrations of the Jewish holy days, such as the weekly Sabbath and the annual Passover, happen around the family table, not in the synagogue. In the Jewish tradition, faith has little meaning unless lived in the home and in the everyday world. The good Jew finds God first of all when the family is gathered together.

Saint Paul and other Jewish leaders in the early church took for granted the basic role of the family as a religious community. We know that long before the early Christians built what could be called a church, they gathered in one another's homes to pray and to celebrate the eucharist. It was families, not isolated individuals, that first heard and responded to the message of God's love and the call to become new people.

Although Jesus seems to have had little to say about family life, in Matthew's gospel he says, "For where two or three are gathered together in my name, there am I in the midst of them" (18:20). It isn't difficult to apply these words to a Christian family. From a Catholic perspective a family is first of all a gathering of some friends and disciples of Jesus.

One of the early saints, John Chrysostom, in the late fourth century called the family "church" (Greek, *ekklesia*). Note well, he did *not* say that the family is "kind of like the church," he said that the family *is* church.

For about the first 1500 years of the church's history, most Christians lived their faith primarily in the everyday-ness of family life. They took it for granted that the family was the most basic form of faith community.

Historically, however, many abuses had arisen within the church which led to the Protestant reformation. In response to the reformation, the church held the Council of Trent (1545-1563) which sealed the division between the Protestant reformers and Catholicism.

At the Council of Trent, the church emphasized institutions and church laws to the neglect of the mysterious nature of faith and the central place of human love in a Christian way of life.

After Trent, during the period known as the counter-reformation, official church laws emphasized the importance of institutional structures and made the parish the center of Catholic life. An official catechism appeared and, in the view of church laws, the parish priest replaced parents as the one ultimately responsible for teaching children about their faith.

Prior to the counter-reformation, an infant to be baptized could have as many godparents as the family wanted to name, including children. This tended to build and nourish relationships with the far-flung clan, on both sides of the family. In the years following Trent, however, church laws limited godparents to one male and one female. Also, the baptism had to be completed within three days of the birth of the child, which meant that unless they lived nearby, aunts and uncles and cousins didn't have time to make the journey.

Although there are understandable reasons for all this, such moves did not help to strengthen family bonds and nourish family faith! Instead, it led to the typical Catholic baptism of the first half of the twentieth century, a small-group, private affair off in a darkened corner of the church with no involvement on the part of the wider parish community.

In the Catholic church that began to take shape in the mid sixteenth century, the parish was the center of religious life, and families were encouraged to draw their basic spiritual sustenance from religious activities based in the parish, not the home. Those devotional activities that did happen at home tended to have a churchy feel to them, and teachers in the church urged married couples to adapt a piety that grew out of the experience of men and women who lived in monasteries.

For such reasons, Catholics lost sight of the truth that the family is an authentic form of faith community. The church forgot that home church and parish church depend upon each other and that *both* need to be lively communities of faith.

In the late nineteenth century, Pope Leo XIII piped up with this remark: "The family was ordained of God . . . it was before the church, or rather the first form of the church on earth." This was a remarkable thing for a pope to say at the time! Unfortunately, however, nothing seems to have come of it until more than half a century later, at the Second Vatican Council (1962-1965).

At Vatican II, the bishops of the world decided not to write a special document on marriage and family life, sensing that marriage and family life are not separate from the church but at its very center. Instead, the bishops wrote about family life in two of the most important council documents, both of which focused on the church as a whole. In these two major documents, the bishops called the family *the domestic church*, reaching back to a tradition nearly forgotten for five hundred years!

It took more than another decade, however, before key people in the church, including theologians and bishops, began to realize the importance of this idea. In the late 1970s, a few theologians and others interested in family life began to study the tradition that the family is a home church. Since then, some important official church documents have appeared. But relatively few Catholics—laity, clergy, and theologians—fully understand the importance of viewing the family as church. People in key positions still need to ask: If the family, in its various forms, is the most basic form the church takes, what does this imply for parish life and for the church at large?

Families—including traditional two-parent families, single-parent families, blended families, childless couples, and parents whose children are grown and gone—are, in the words of Pope John Paul II, meant to "constitute the church in its fundamental dimension." This is a truth that has only just begun to have an impact on Catholics. But it is an idea that contains the seeds of new life.

The family, in its various forms, is meant to be a genuine community of faith. Christ calls each family to love and serve one another in ways appropriate to families. Sometimes when family people hear this, however, they jump to strange conclusions. Here's one example.

A speaker at a workshop for parents asked the participants to raise their hands if in the last week they had fed the hungry. No hands. Clothed the naked? No hands. Comforted the lonely? Still no response. Except way in the back of the room a tentative hand went up. A woman in her mid-thirties stood and hesitantly said, "Well, um, I guess you could say that I sort of do those things everyday with my three young children . . . sort of . . . I guess . . ."

Bingo! And not just "sort of," either! We parents are engaged in a full-fledged, full-scale Christian ministry, not some backwater, unimportant activity. Raising children, with its many joys and sacrifices, failures and triumphs, is smack at the middle of what the church is about.

Of course, Christ also calls families to show an active concern for those outside their immediate family who have special needs. Families do this in many ways, but always so that their involvements nourish their family, not add to its stresses. It is important for families to find ways to serve the less fortunate that nourish their own family life, not harm it. After all, what good is it to do something for someone else if it causes our own family members to love one another less?

Family prayer and ritual is important to a family's life together. The key here is for the family to learn to pray and participate in home rituals in ways that are natural to family life. Formal prayer and ritual forms that make perfectly good sense in church generally do not work well at home.

Christ calls families to place love of God and neighbor at the center of their lives. This means that we must try to ignore messages which tell us to think of our own comfort and security first. We need to constantly ask ourselves if our home life is shaped more by the gospel or by commercial messages that constantly urge us to be dissatisfied with what we have.

Married couples, who are the smallest form of genuine Christian community have a special vocation to be the founders and guides of families. We husbands and wives are meant to be a special sign of God's love and faithfulness in the world, and we will be this sign if we do all we can to keep our marriages happy and healthy. Remember, too, that parenthood as a full-time occupation is temporary. We need to nurture our marriage regularly so that when our children no longer need us as mom and dad, our marriage will still be healthy.

To parents, married or single, belongs the most important teaching authority in the church. We teach our children by word and example what it means to be a follower of Christ and a member of the Christian community. If we parents don't do our job well, teachings from church authorities will fall on deaf ears. Therefore, parents are, indeed, the most important channels of Catholic tradition to the next generation.

The relationship between the parish church and a home church, or family, is an especially important one. For each depends upon the other to be its own best self. In order for the parish to be an authentic faith community, families must be strong faith communities. Much as the basic cells in the human body must be healthy in order for the entire body to be sound, then the households that constitute the parish must be healthy in order for the parish community to be all that it is meant to be.

At the same time, the Christian households that constitute the parish need the support of the parish community in order to remain healthy and strong. It is important for parish priests and lay ministers to have an active concern for nourishing family life in its various forms. For the place most of us encounter God most frequently is in our marriages and families.

This is why the relationship between the parish and the families that make up the parish is called interdependent, because each depends upon the other. If our parishes and their leaders nourish and support families, the parish will be a lively, dynamic community of faith. And if we strive to make our families genuine faith communities, our parish can't help but be a credit to the gospel and to the church as a whole.

In the not too distant future, many parishes will have to get by without a priest in residence. As this begins to happen, married couples will become more and more important as leaders of small groups of Catholic and interfaith families who will gather regularly for spiritual, educational, and social purposes. In this sense, married couples will become leaders of critical importance to the future of Catholicism.

Christian families, then, are the church's most basic cell, and a primary thrust of church life should be to nourish and support family life in all its dimensions.

FAMILY FOCAL POINT 1

Pope John Paul II, in his 1981 "Apostolic Exhortation on the Family," says that the first mission of a Christian family is to "become more and more what it is, that is, a community of life and love." He insists that a family "has the mission to guard, reveal and communicate love." And a family's love "is a real sharing in God's love."

The pope outlines four general tasks for a Christian family: 1) to form a true community of persons; 2) to serve life; 3) to participate in constructive ways in the life of the wider society; and 4) to share in the life and mission of the church at large.

To form a true community of persons, says the pope, a family has only to dedicate itself to love. "Without love the family is not a community of persons and, in the same way, without love the family cannot live, grow, and perfect itself as a community of persons." Indeed, people "cannot live without love."

To serve life, especially by giving birth to and raising children in a loving environment, is "the fundamental task" of the traditional nuclear family. This includes the spiritual life that parents pass on to their children. Thus, families should guard against being imprisoned by "a consumer mentality," and should oppose government policies that undermine family life. Parents, says the pope, should help their children to learn that people are more important for what they are than for what they have.

To participate in constructive ways in the life of the wider society, says John Paul II, is basic to Christian family life. But the first way families do this is by living together in a way that allows love to thrive in the family itself. In this way, families become a "school of social life, an example and stimulus for the broader community of relationships marked by respect, justice, dialogue, and love."

Insofar as it is a small-scale church, a family is called upon, "like the large-scale church, to be a sign of unity for the world . . . by bearing witness to the kingdom and peace of Christ, toward which the whole world is journeying."

To share in the life and mission of the church at large does not mean that families should spend large blocks of time with parish organizations and activities. Rather, prior to any such involvements a family is a "church in miniature . . . a living image and historical representation of the mystery of the church."

As a domestic church, a family shares in the life and mission of the wider church by being a community of life and love, by praying together in ways suited to family life, and by developing family rituals to celebrate God's presence in the many ordinary and special events that mark the liturgical year and punctuate a family's daily existence.

Finally, a family participates in the wider mission of the church by practicing "love in all its relationships, so that it does not live closed in on itself, but remains open to the community, moved by a sense of justice and concern for others, as well as by a consciousness of its responsibility toward the whole of society."

Families have a special mission, says the pope, to teach the church as a whole how to love. "Thanks to love within the family, the church can and ought to take on a more homelike or family dimension, developing a more human and fraternal style of relationships."

FAMILY FOCAL POINT 2

Mixed or interfaith marriages, in which one spouse is Catholic while the other professes a Protestant or non-Christian religion, have a vocation with a special dimension. They are called to express in their homes and in their lives together an openness—built on respect—to one another's religious traditions. It can be a rich experience for children to grow up in an interfaith home, learning to appreciate their parents' two religious traditions.

In his excellent book, *Beginning Your Marriage*, Rev. John L. Thomas, S.J., makes some practical suggestions for interfaith couples. Here are five of them:

- Encourage your partner in his or her religious pursuits and practices. . . . Since these practices will help each partner become his or her best self, they can only enrich and benefit your relationship.

- Attend each other's worship services occasionally. Try to understand the experience and tradition from which your partner's faith life has come. . . .

- . . . Learn to pray together with some regularity. Pray about your lives, your hopes and needs; pray for the people dear to you, for those in great need and about some of the critical questions facing all of us today. . . .

Maybe you could use some prayer formulas from each partner's tradition. . . .

- Consider subscribing to a quality publication put out by each of your faith traditions and buy some books . . . on religious themes. . . .

- Find some charitable or service-oriented projects for the poor, the aged, children, etc. which you could undertake together in order to give expression to your faith commitment.

CHAPTER 4

Catholic Families
Are Gospel Communities

NOT LONG AFTER MY WIFE KATHY and I were first married, we moved to a distant city neither of us had ever seen before. It took several days to drive there, our meager earthly belongings in tow. Once we arrived, however, one of the first things we did was to locate what would be our parish.

We were impressed by the spirit of this inner city community. Mass each Sunday morning jumped with participation; there were few, if any, mere spectators. The parish also sponsored a hot meal program six nights a week that fed hundreds of people and involved teams from all over the metropolitan area.

What was most important for us, however, was that our new parish brought genuinely Christian families into our life as a young married couple. From them we learned that to have a healthy marriage and family meant having the courage and fortitude to swim upstream.

One family in particular taught us, by example far more than by words, that people and time with one another is what really matters.

Bob and Karen had seven children ranging in age from eight to nineteen. Bob helped his brother run a tool distributorship, Karen worked part-time in the kitchen at a convalescent home. Their house was old, as were the furniture and appliances. You would have to say that this was a home that had been well lived-in.

From the first time we visited Bob and Karen and their children we hardly noticed their house, however. What we saw and felt was a family we could admire. There was a real sense of "what you see is what you get." Bob and Karen felt no need to pretend to be perfect, they made no apologies for the banged up dining room table and the worn spot on the kitchen floor's linoleum. They offered only a sense of "welcome to our family. How about helping us put together ravioli from scratch?"

In this family, table prayer was from the heart, no rushed-through formality or pietistic production. Sunday dinner was a nearly chaotic family festival. Children of every size tumbled into chairs of every description. Visitors were served first, and several conversations collided in midair as the meal lurched along toward groans of satisfaction and looser belts.

This family was holy—hale and hearty—not perfect. They had their problems, including a son who had to be claimed one night from a sojourn in a police station. They told the tale with regret but they also said, "That's the way it goes, that's life for you sometimes." Bob and Karen did not pretend that they had perfect kids, but they insisted on loving them and doing their best to help them become happy, responsible adults.

When Kathy and I began to have children of our own, we knew from personal observation of families like Bob's and Karen's that our future depended on our willingness to give top priority to people and caring relationships. Gradually, we learned that to strive to live this ideal would demand risks and a readiness to be different.

The gospel invites Christian families to a different way of life and each family responds in unique ways. Some sense a call to live as simply as possible, to care little for having new furniture and a fashionable wardrobe. Some reject the idea of buying children toy guns and other war toys. Because of social pressures, being such a family is difficult, but the rewards are many. Children understand peace as a value, and when they feel loved and cared for they place less importance on superficial things.

The mass media saturates us with the idea that possessions can buy peace of mind and warm family relationships. It pummels our senses with the propaganda that we will be happy if we earn enough money and buy the *right* house, car, clothes, and toys, use the *right* antiperspirant and makeup, buy the *right* personal computer, and invest in a big enough insurance policy.

So all-pervasive is this attitude that we tend to see no contradiction between what we see and hear on television and what we see and hear in church on Sundays. Our hearts often are numb to what the gospels really say.

We tend to think that Christian faith has a merely abstract meaning, and the teachings and traditions of the church have little to do with the real world. We tend to believe that Christianity is about nothing more than being nice to other people, saying our prayers, and getting into heaven after we die.

Kathy and I learned three things from Bob and Karen and other families that we have known since then. First, we learned that happiness and a healthy family do not come from trying to become as comfortable and financially secure as possible.

The *hale and hearty* family we want comes more from spending time with family members than from spending money on them. Sure, we need to earn a livelihood. But there is no need to be forever worrying about making more and more money in order to buy more and more stuff. (What a relief!)

In Matthew's gospel, Jesus puts it this way:

. . . do not worry about your life, what you will eat [or drink], or about your body, what you will wear. . . . Can any of you by worrying add a single moment to your life span? . . . So do not worry. . . (6:25-31).

Second, families like Bob's and Karen's taught us that Christianity is not a Sunday religious formality, it's a challenging, enriching way of life, seven days a week, every day of the month, 365 days a year.

To say we are a Catholic family means that we will do our best to love one another daily. If work and outside activities begin to deprive us of family time together, we will talk and pray together and make whatever sacrifices are needed in order to regain control.

At the same time, we will try to pay more attention to scripture and the traditions of the church and less attention to empty but seductive commercial messages. We can do without ads that imply that we are shameful parents if we do not earn more money in order to buy more stuff. Consumerism, the philosophy which insists that human fulfillment comes from a lifelong buying spree, wants us always to be dissatisfied with what we already have. But the good news is that we can choose to resist any such suggestion. We believe that we are created to love one another, not to go shopping.

In Matthew's gospel, Jesus puts it this way:

> No one can serve two masters. He will either hate one and love the other, or be devoted to one and despise the other. You cannot serve God and mammon (6:24).

Third, we learned that the Catholic way of life is about constantly learning and re-learning how to give our whole heart, in love, to God and to those knockabout people with whom we live and work. We learned that to spend time with spouse and children is to spend time with God, too. And to "spend time with" is to love.

In our family, we try to do this by working less and being home more. We also place much importance on doing things together. When one son has a basketball game, as many family members as possible attend. When another son is in a spelling bee, we are there to chew our nails and cheer him on.

We have a tradition during the summer months of attending baseball games together. After mass on Sundays, we pick up donuts to have at home, and on Friday evenings we like to pop a big bowl of popcorn and listen to stories, either from a public radio broadcast or recordings from the public library. Such traditions help to hold a family together and counter the pressures of society that tend to pull families apart.

In Luke's gospel, Jesus puts it this way:

> You shall love the Lord, your God, with all your heart, with all your being, with all your strength, and with all your mind, and your neighbor as yourself (10:27).

From our Catholic perspective, a healthy family lifestyle must be rooted in the high priestly prayer of Jesus in the gospel of John. Before he is to die, Jesus prays to the Father:

> And now I will no longer be in the world, but they [his disciples, including us] are in the world. . . . I do not ask you to take them out of the world but that you keep them from the evil one. They do not belong to the world any more than I belong to the world (17:11-16).

What this means for families is that Christ calls us to live in and for the world, serving and caring for one another. *But,* Christ calls us to do this in a way that the world sometimes does not understand or approve.

This is where we get down to brass tacks. When we stress loving relationships and spending plenty of time on family, we often must say no to other points of view. We must say no to a world that insists that a healthy family comes from a constant anxious concern for a more and more comfortable lifestyle and an ever-increasing level of financial security.

Of course, living "in but not of the world" means different things for different families. Here are two stories about two unique families to show what I mean. These stories are true, although I have changed the names and some of the details to conceal real identities.

Donna was a divorced mother of three young children. After her divorce was finalized, she could barely drag herself out of bed each morning, she was feeling so low. She went through her day's work, as a bank teller, depressed and fearful about the future. She also felt guilty for having to leave her children in a low-cost day-care home that she suspected did not give her children the attention they needed.

Donna had been away from the church for years, but she began to pray each night that God would help her to find a way out of her depression. Then she met Sharon, a woman she had known in high school, who belonged to a support group for divorced Catholics. After hearing Donna's story, Sharon invited her to join the group's weekly lunch meeting at a fast-food restaurant.

Over the course of several weeks, Donna found in this small Catholic group a healthy faith perspective on her life, and soon returned to the church. An important part of what Donna learned was that she needed to trust in God's love enough to not allow fear and anxiety to control her life.

Sharon encouraged her. "You're doing okay, Donna. Stop and take a look. You're a good mom, your children are getting along fine, and you got a letter from your supervisor praising your work, which means you'll probably get a promotion one of these days."

Slowly, and with the help of a wise counselor, Donna began to realize that the less she gave in to her anxiety and the more she relied on the love of God, the more energy she had to care for her children and the happier she was with her work. Donna didn't learn to let go of her fear overnight, of course. But she discovered the wisdom of trying daily to put her own peace of mind and her love for her children in first place. She began to learn the wisdom of relying on God from one day to the next. This is what living "in but not of the world" meant for Donna in the real circumstances of her life.

Another family, with teen-age children, found in their faith the light they needed to get to know one another again, but not without much pain and anguish.

Rich and Carolyn were a thoroughly upscale couple. They had been married for twenty years, and they had two bright and popular daughters. Rich was a doctor with a highly successful family practice, Carolyn was an attorney who specialized in medical malpractice cases.

This family had everything society tells us we need to be happy: a big, comfortable home loaded with all the new appliances, expensive furniture, and entertainment gadgets. They had plenty of money, late model cars, and the "in" clothing fashions. But something was very wrong.

In the last few years, Rich had been drinking too much, and Carolyn had become involved on the sly with another man. If Rich and Carolyn were good at anything, however, they were good at keeping up appearances. The family still attended mass together every Sunday.

The daughters, who were seventeen and fifteen, were the envy of their classmates. They always had plenty of spending money so they didn't have to find after-school jobs, their closets were full of new clothes, and they drove to school in a sporty looking car their father had bought for them when the oldest girl got her driver's license.

The daughters had their troubles, too, however. Both had started drinking, experimenting with drugs, and the oldest was sexually involved with her boyfriend.

At their infrequent family dinners, Rich and Carolyn and the girls hardly spoke to one another. Painful fights and shouting-matches happened almost every day. No one ever said so, but each of them preferred to be anyplace but at home.

Rich and Carolyn were miserable and they knew it, but they didn't know what to do about it. Call it the grace of God or call it chance, but one Sunday the married deacon in their parish delivered a homily about family life that rattled them both. You might say that it knocked them for a cosmic loop.

The gospel reading was about a man who found a treasure buried in a field, buried the treasure again, then went and sold everything he owned in order to buy that field. (See Matthew 13:44.) The deacon compared the treasure to a healthy marriage and family life and said that as friends and followers of Christ we should be willing to give up everything the world can offer in order to have such a treasure. Not only that, he said, but those who don't do this lay out the welcome mat for misery and grief. For lasting joy comes from loving and caring for one another.

Rich and Carolyn knew what the deacon meant by misery and grief. That night in bed they cried in one another's arms, and two days later they cleared their packed calendars to get together with a skilled, caring, no-nonsense family therapist. In the end, Rich's and Carolyn's Catholic roots had enough life left in them to help save their marriage and family. With much effort, not a few tears, and plenty of talking and listening, the parents and daughters eventually got to know one another again.

Rich cut back on his practice to the point that he now takes off one week every two months, plus a three-week vacation each summer. Carolyn had the good fortune of being able to cut back her hours at the law firm to four days a week. The two daughters began to enjoy being at home again, and with help from a counselor they retreated from the brink of dangerous drugs and unhealthy sexual involvements.

This is a dramatic story of a family that learned what

it means for Christian families to live "in but not of the world." As Catholic families, we shoot for this goal: to love God and one another above everything else, and to realize that whatever obstructs this project deserves the old heave-ho.

FAMILY FOCAL POINT

Advertisers know that we crave warm family relationships today, but they also know how tough these are to come by. Magazine ads and TV commercials use words and images from family life to sell us everything from beer to cars, from insurance policies to typewriters. Buy these things, they clearly imply, and your craving for a warm, healthy family life will be met.

Banks and insurance companies have for many years appealed to "trust," "fidelity," and "your loved ones" to sell their services. Endless ordinary eateries in recent years suddenly became "family restaurants." In an era when grandparents and grandchildren tend to see one another infrequently, a bank ad shows a boy and his grandfather fishing from a row boat—only this and the name of the bank. Auto manufacturers routinely portray ecstatic families gathered in front of a new station wagon or van. "Welcome," says an ad for a van, "to our new family room."

None of these products or services have much to do with family life, of course. The only way we can have a healthy, rewarding family life is to spend time with one another, talking, playing, working, and praying.

CHAPTER 5

Keeping Your Marriage Happy and Healthy

YEARS AGO, WHEN KATHY AND I were a young engaged couple, fresh-faced and bursting with joy at the mere fact of each other's existence, we met an old man. Neatly attired in a dark three-piece suit, he smiled at us one Sunday morning after mass, extended both his hands so that each of us could hold one, and asked if we were in love.

I remember thinking, "Oh brother, here we go." I felt like we were about to launch into a scene from some romantic 1950s movie, as if the old man were looking for an excuse to sing, "Hello, Young Lovers." But he simply smiled and held our hands for a moment, and after we acknowledged that we were engaged he said something I've never forgotten.

"Listen," he confided. "Listen. My wife just died a couple of months ago, and do you know what occurred to me the other day? I'll tell you. A marriage license is nothing but a learner's permit. That's right, nothing but a learner's permit." The old man laughed quietly, wished us well, and said goodbye.

A couple of months later, we began to learn to be married, and we are still learning today. Recalling the old man's words recently, I said to Kathy, "I guess a married couple can't say that their marriage is a success until one spouse is dead and gone!"

"No," Kathy replied, "I don't think so. I think a marriage is successful as long as both spouses keep on trying to learn to be married well. When it comes to marriage, success isn't arriving at a destination, success is the journey itself."

She's correct and there are certain ideas that a couple can keep in mind to help them stay on the right road with a minimum number of detours.

First, and probably most basic today, is the fact that in the last couple of generations marriage has changed. It used to be that most people agreed on what was "men's work," and what was "women's work." But no more. In fact, everything is up for grabs so that each couple must make decisions that suit them best.

When Bill and Julie married recently, they got plenty of advice from their respective parents. Bill's father told him that it was all well and good for he and Julie to want to share everything equally in their marriage, including money, possessions, and decision-making. "But," he pontificated, index finger raised in the air, "sooner or later somebody has to wear the pants in the family." The idea was, of course, that Bill had better learn to take charge, and Julie had better learn to do as she was told.

Bill felt exasperated. He and Julie talked it over and decided that they disagreed with Bill's father. "We both will wear the pants in this family," they agreed.

Marriage today is different from marriage as earlier generations knew it. A man and woman still vow to love each other in good times and bad, in sickness and in health, until death. But the ways husband and wife interpret and apply these words have been changing dramatically for some time. The world is changing as is marriage.

When the parents of Bill and Julie married, it was still common for women with children to stay home full-time. Today Julie plans to work outside the home, even after she and Bill have children. Bill's father never changed a diaper, but Bill has every intention of fully participating in the care of their children. Julie's mother did all the cooking and cleaning; Julie and Bill agree that they want to share such things as equally as they can. It wouldn't be fair, they think, for Julie to bear full responsibility for meals and housework when she spends as much time working outside the home as Bill does.

Marriage is gradually becoming a union of equals. Couples are less and less comfortable with a male-dominant approach. Instead, they want to face life together as friends and companions, each supporting and depending upon the other.

The second point is that marriage is most likely to succeed when the man and woman who marry have managed to do a lot of growing up beforehand. Most of us grow up and get married, of course. But the problem is that we don't always do it in that order.

One of the main reasons marriages of people under twenty-one have a high rate of failure is that it is terribly difficult for anyone to give himself or herself to another until the issue of who I am has been settled. I can't give away a self that I haven't discovered or developed yet.

When Moira and Carl first met, he was twenty-eight, she was twenty-six. Both had finished college, done some traveling, and answered some basic questions for themselves about the meaning and purpose of life. They recognized that they shared a firm belief in living for others and in cultivating a simple way of life. Neither was interested in becoming wealthy and both wanted to work with and for people with special needs. Their faith was important to both, and was much more than a nice thing to do on Sunday mornings.

Moira and Carl felt good about their decision to marry because they shared the same basic values and attitudes. They believed that they were sent into the world to love each other and their children first of all, and that life has no meaning apart from faithfulness to this project. Since they agreed on this they felt they could trust in God to help other important but secondary matters take care of themselves.

This young couple also agreed that the word "divorce" would not be in their vocabulary; in their marriage divorce would never be an option as a way to resolve differences between them. For Moira and Carl, a lifetime together is what it's about. Period.

The third point is that marriage is a process. The only thing that can be counted on to remain unchanged is that things will always be changing.

Mary Beth and Steve have been married for fourteen years, and they have two children, a ten-year-old boy and an eight-year-old girl. When they talk about their marriage, they remark on how different they are today, as individuals and as a couple.

"When we got married," Mary Beth says, "I thought we would both keep doing the kind of work we were doing then. I was teaching, Steve was a counselor in a drug addiction treatment program. We've each been through two jobs since then, with time out for further education. We had babies who are now children in school. We moved twice, and both of us are older. You don't have to convince me that change is what marriage is all about!"

Steve and Mary Beth are still the same people they were when they got married, but in sharing change they have grown and changed as persons, so in some ways they're different. Throughout their years together they have had to stay in touch as two growing, changing individuals who promised to stay together and love each other for a lifetime. "Hey!" says Steve. "We even *look* different. For example, when we got married I had a thick, full head of hair. . ."

Which leads to the fourth point. Healthy marriage requires time. Someone once said that a marriage is like a little child, it needs to be picked up and hugged and given plenty of tender loving care.

When Kathy and I were first married, we decided that we would set aside regular times for just the two of us, to enjoy each other, to talk, to have fun. Prior to the birth of our first child, this was not difficult. We made time for each other spontaneously. At the drop of a hat, we would decide to go out for dinner, see a movie, attend a special lecture, see a play, or simply go for a walk in a park.

Along came our first child, however, and life got more complicated. Two weeks after our son's birth, we summoned up our courage and promised each other that we would get a baby-sitter one night a week in order to go out for the evening. We have done that for nearly twenty years, now.

It borders on the unreasonable to expect a marriage to survive long periods of being taken for granted. Different couples give their marriages time in different ways, however. George and Rita pop popcorn each evening after their kids are in bed. Then they turn off the TV set and talk. Sometimes they play cards or a board game.

"It became clear a couple of years ago," George says, "that television was robbing us of time in the evening when we could really be present for each other. We decided that our marriage is more important than getting a few yucks from some goofy sitcom."

John and Barbara take off for a whole weekend every month. They hire a trusted sitter or drop their two boys with willing grandparents and leave town. "Sure," John says, "this costs money, and sometimes we can't afford it but we do it anyway. It's a question of priorities. Some people use their money to buy new furniture and stuff like that, or they save up to buy a boat or go to Europe. We use our money to enjoy each other's company (which is the main reason people get married!) and to stay in touch."

Item five is that it's important for spouses to remain

healthy as individuals, too. A man and woman don't usually get married unless they find each other to be interesting individuals. As time goes by, however, spouses tend to think they've heard everything the other has to say. To head boredom off at the pass, husband and wife need to do whatever they can to remain interesting to be with, not only for their own sakes but for the sake of their marriage.

Once a year, Kathy and I give each other the gift of a six-day retreat at a monastery. We believe that it's good for our marriage for each of us to have this time for spiritual enrichment. Indeed, one of the best presents a spouse can give his or her partner is some time to attend to the inner life.

Richard and Clara agree with this, but they encourage each other to grow as individuals in other ways, too. Richard kisses Clara out the door one evening each week so she can indulge her enthusiasm for calligraphy. Clara, for her part, supports Richard's weekly evening playing basketball.

Bob and Judy enjoy bowling together, but they also have interests the other does not share. Judy sings in a parish choir, Bob likes to tinker with cars, so they gladly offer each other regular times to pursue these individual interests.

Marriage is like juggling. Couples need to spend time together regularly, but they need to allow each other individual time, too. It's a matter of trying to keep several balls in the air, two of which are labeled "couple time" and "individual time." If they drop one ball, their marriage will suffer.

Item six is this: Marriage today requires practical skills. For a marriage to stay healthy, husband and wife need to gain some basic communication skills and learn how to deal with their differences in ways that will strengthen, not weaken, their relationship. Some couples do this by enrolling in a workshop on marital communication, others read and discuss a good book on the topic. Attending a Marriage Encounter weekend can be a move in the right direction, too.

We had a friend, Phyllis (now deceased), who was a wife of many years, a mother of four grown offspring, and a wise marriage counselor. One autumn day, Kathy and I invited her to help us give an evening workshop for married couples. When it came time for Phyllis to give her presentation, she stood up and said: "In order for a couple to resolve their differences in ways that will help their marriage, they must want to be married more than they want to be right."

We should never expect marriage to be conflict-free. Instead, we must accept conflict as an opportunity to resolve differences in order to draw closer together. It's necessary to face up to the pain of our differences in order to know the joy of a deeper love. Sometimes, indeed, this means having the good sense to get some help from a qualified marriage counselor. It's not much different from seeing a doctor for help with a sore throat.

This brings me to point seven, which I think is especially important. I don't believe any couple can hope to have a happy, lasting marriage unless they share some form of religious faith. Studies certainly show that the divorce rate is much lower among such couples.

Kathy and I gladly testify to the fact that our marriage benefits in endless ways from our participation in the church's spiritual, social, and educational activities. We find in the Catholic church a great deal of support for our marriage. At home we celebrate the religious roots of the seasons of Advent, Christmas, Lent, and Easter. We pray around our table each evening, as a family. We also find special nourishment for our marriage when we join our parish community to celebrate the eucharist on Sundays and when we receive communion together.

So central is faith in a Catholic marriage that official church teaching many centuries ago declared that marriage is a sacrament. In a nutshell, this means that in their patient and passionate love for each other, husband and wife know God's love, too.

When Carlos and Maria married twenty-five years ago, they got the impression that marriage as a sacrament simply meant that they received a sacrament at their wedding, a kind of special one-shot dose of grace. Along the way, however, they learned otherwise.

"It's really quite amazing," Maria says. "We know today that I experience God's love most often in Carlos' love for me, and vice versa. This is true of the ordinary, everyday ways we love each other, but it's true in a special way when we make love. Carlos and I are called by God to be grace for each other. That's what it means to say that marriage is a sacrament."

I sometimes startle married couples when I talk about how important loving sexual intimacy is in a Christian marriage. The truth is that the Holy Spirit dances and plays gracefully in the lovemaking of any ordinary, imperfect, marriage. Without the pleasures of the marriage bed (to put it quaintly) husbands and wives would be deprived of a vital source of grace that binds and renews their marriage time after time.

Experts on marital sexuality sometimes compare making love to enjoying a special meal together. If we borrow this image, in most marriages there are more trips to fast food places than there are leisurely dinners at a high-class restaurant. All the same, whenever I talk to groups of married couples, I insist that God nourishes the love of husband and wife even through their most ordinary lovemaking.

In a very real sense making love is a kind of "holy communion." So important is loving sexual intimacy to a Christian couple that marriage is almost impossible without a happy sexual adjustment. Of course, sexual adjustment all by itself does not guarantee a happy marriage, but it sure helps!

A newly-wed couple once approached me during a break in a workshop I was giving on Christian marriage. I could tell from their politely puzzled expressions that they had a question.

"We were wondering," the young man asked, "if you could tell us in just a few words what the difference is between a Christian marriage and one that is not Christian."

I thought for a moment, then said: "What makes the difference is that in a Christian marriage husband and wife look first to scripture and the ancient and modern traditions of the church for guidance on how to live their life together. They know that God can be trusted to renew and heal their love each and every day, even when the going gets difficult. In a secular marriage, the couple is probably going to be guided more by what's popular and socially acceptable than anything else, and for them God may be only a kind of last resort rather than a daily companion."

Later, as the workshop continued, I repeated what I had said to this couple. Then I added: "A Christian marriage is meant to be a triangle: a man, a woman, and God. Ah, but that's not the best image to use, for so intimate is God with husband and wife that their love for one another brings them into union with God."

Perhaps the First Letter of John says it best, in words that carry a special meaning for married couples: ". . . if we love one another, God remains in us, and his love is brought to perfection in us" (4:12).

FAMILY FOCAL POINT 1

Many couples who marry in the church today do not share the same faith. While mixed faith couples have unique challenges to face in their marriages, they also have unique opportunities to enrich their life together and special gifts to offer their children.

It is essential for spouses in mixed marriages to respect each other's faith and religious tradition. Regardless of how they resolve the issue of which community to join on Sundays, spouses can blend their two traditions in their own home and help their children to appreciate both.

At the same time, however, couples in mixed marriages should realize that any marriage is mixed to one degree or another. For example, Anthony grew up in a big, Italian Catholic family. His wife Maria's parents are second generation Catholic Mexican-Americans. Anthony and Maria are both Catholic, but talk about their religious differences!

Stu is Jewish, Teresa is Catholic, and they offer this bit of advice for any interfaith couple: "Respect, respect, respect. Talk, talk, talk. And love each other a lot."

FAMILY FOCAL POINT 2

In their book *Marital Intimacy: A Catholic Perspective*, John Meyer Anzia and Mary G. Durkin suggest that a marriage is constantly in a spiral process. There are, say the authors, four phases: falling in love, settling down, bottoming out, and beginning again, a process that happens over and over.

Falling in love is easy to understand, but sometimes couples don't realize that the ease with which they love at such times is a special grace from God. It's just a hint, say Anzia and Durkin, of what God has in store for couples who continue to cultivate their love for each other.

Settling down is just that, the rut couples tend to slip into as they cope with life in the real world.

Bottoming out happens in different ways for different couples. For some, it really is a major case of the pits, involving much pain and anguish. For others, it may be little more than a sense of boredom or a feeling that things just aren't right for them. Moving from this phase to the next one requires trust in God and the willingness to give in to grace and respond to the attractiveness of the other.

Beginning again requires the courage to ask each other for the comfort and understanding we need. This phase, too, demands faith and trust that God's love is at work in our marriage.

Couples, say Durkin and Anzia, should never listen to marital prophets of doom. No marriage is destined to be a dull routine. Rather, we can become lovers if we accept that "down times" in marriage are but invitations to once again respond to each other with a love that is both patient and passionate. When we do this, before long we find ourselves falling in love once again.

CHAPTER 6

Parenting in a Christian Context

SOME YEARS AGO, COLUMNIST Ann Landers asked her readers to write her about their experience as parents. If you had the chance to choose again, she wanted to know, would you have children? Much to her surprise, the great majority of the thousands who answered her question said no, they would not have children if they could choose again.

Landers admitted in a subsequent column that she was shocked. "For heaven's sake," she said, "if you didn't have children what would you do with your life?" As far as she was concerned, being a parent is one of life's most important callings. After all, where would the world be without parents?

If Ann Landers' survey reveals anything, it's that parenthood is no picnic. Moms and dads put up with a lot of inconvenience and irritation and often get little thanks for their trouble. At the same time, however, the potential rewards of being parents are great. Sometimes the following quip rings true: "The only thing worse than having children is not having children."

Parents ask many questions about their offspring and how to raise them, but all of them can be distilled into one basic question: How can we raise children who will grow up to be good people?

Tim and Alice are a good example of a young couple

who learned the basic answer to this question. Five years ago, when these two said "I do," they had no idea that within a couple of years they would be the parents of twin girls. They also did not have a clue that the cornerstone of effective parenting has little to do with what we can read in books.

"Here's what it boils down to," Tim says: "What matters most in being a good parent is the parents growing up themselves. Before people have babies they need to know who they are and what they believe in, and they need to be able to make a decent living."

Tim's point is that children need mature, well-adjusted parents more than anything else. This doesn't always happen and even when it does, children have a way of bringing out their parents' weaknesses in a hurry. As someone said, there's nothing like a four-year-old to make a parent act like a three-year-old. Still, the ideal is for parents to grow up and act like adults.

Here is what I mean:

- When babies stretch parents' energy and patience to the breaking point, the most important thing for parents to have is maturity and self-control.

- When little children or teen-agers ask questions about their bodies, or about sexual intimacy, the most important thing for parents to have is a high level of comfort with their own sexuality.

- When children misbehave, the most important thing for parents to be able to do is to act more grown-up than their children. Given this maturity, attending a class on parenting can be a good idea. (It's also true that such a class can help parents become more grown-up.)

- When children want to pour the milk themselves, or cross the street alone, parents need to know when the time is right and how to feel secure enough to let go. And such self-assurance can only be gained by growing up oneself.

Tom and Marilyn are the parents of a six-week-old girl. "I need more sleep!" Marilyn says. "And when can Tom and I have an evening to ourselves? Is this how it's going to be for the next twenty years? Interrupted sleep and no marriage? Ack!"

"Hey," Tom adds, "sometimes I wonder if our apartment is going to smell like diapers and baby powder permanently!"

Marilyn and Tom are kidding, but only a little. Their questions are important. And one of the best sources they can turn to is experienced parents.

Fortunately, Tom and Marilyn belong to a parish that offers new parents the opportunity to get together with older, more experienced parents. Frank and Gwen have helped Tom and Marilyn maintain a healthy perspective on their situation and a sense of humor.

Gwen and Frank "volunteered" one of their teen-age daughters to babysit for Tom and Marilyn one evening and invited them over for dinner. Gwen and Frank listened more than anything else and sympathized with Tom's and Marilyn's situation. They were tempted to give in to the "just you wait" pitfall, as in: "Just you wait until your kids are teen-agers; you think you have problems now!" But they successfully resisted because they knew that such remarks wouldn't help.

Gwen recalled her own countless nights of fractured sleep and passed along her advice to Marilyn to "sleep when the baby does." Frank encouraged Tom to help more with midnight feedings and counseled the young couple to establish a bedtime for their baby and stick to it. "The baby may cry the first few times," Frank said, "but before long she'll get the hint that bedtime is at seven o'clock. Remember, the two of you need time to yourselves in the evening."

Frank and Gwen also advised Tom and Marilyn that one of the best investments they could make in their marriage and in their effectiveness as parents, was getting out together about one evening a week.

"Babies are very adaptable little creatures," Gwen said. "They get along fine with a variety of adults. So cultivate a regular sitter and make whatever financial sacrifices are necessary to get out once a week together. The little one may be at the stage where she'll hang on to your pantleg as you head out the door. She'll cry and wail, 'Don't leave me, Mommy!' And when that happens, you have to think, 'Hey, I'm doing this as much for your sake as mine, kid.'"

The stages of childhood correspond to the stages of parenting. First we parent babies, then young children, then middle years children, and finally adolescents. Certain principles and ideals apply no matter what ages our children may be.

Probably the most basic task parents have is to nurture in their children from day one the feeling that they are loved and cherished. Experts on childrearing call it "building positive self-esteem."

Why is this important? Because nothing is more fundamental to becoming a good, mature, healthy adult than the bedrock sense that I am a good and worthwhile person.

Child psychologists point out that children who have a positive, healthy regard for themselves will trust their own feelings and inclinations when it comes to making important decisions and will be much less at risk when it comes to peer pressure.

Also, teens who know they are loved and worthwhile are much less likely to get involved with drugs or sex.

The classic book on this topic is *Your Child's Self-Es-*

teem, by Dorothy Corkille Briggs, and the author summarizes the point of her book herself: "... if your child has *high self-esteem*, he [or she] has it made."

The goal is not to encourage the child to be self-centered or narcissistic. In fact, a self-centered adult probably suffers from a lack of positive self-esteem. The point is to help the child become secure enough to be able to abandon concern for self and be interested in the welfare of others.

From a Catholic perspective there is more to high self-esteem than feeling good about oneself. In fact, a healthy sense of self has a basic religious dimension. When a child feels that he or she is lovable and worthwhile, we say that this is a basic experience of God's love, too. "I am good because God made me and loves me."

Maggie, the mother of two adopted children, put it this way: "When I hug my kids and tell them that I love them and Daddy loves them, I believe I'm channeling God's love to them as well. That's what parents are, it seems to me: a way for God to show children that they are loved with an endless, unconditional love."

Not only do parents communicate God's love to their children, they actually shape their children's image of God. If we call God "Father," children need a warm and loving experience of their own father for that image to make sense. If a child's experience of a father is unpleasant or, perhaps, nonexistent, it doesn't do much good to tell that child that God is a loving Father.

On the other hand, it's never prudent to underestimate children. One young man, whose father was far from the ideal loving parent, said this: "My father was not a good father. But I knew that, and I used to dream about what a good father would be like, and I knew that was what God would be like. I remember thinking, when I was about ten years old, that God was not like my father, God was just the opposite, full of love and totally accepting of me."

According to Briggs, the primary way parents can nourish positive self-esteem in their babies and young children is to give them lots of physical affection—plenty of hugs—and the right kinds of "word messages."

Hugs are easy to understand, but what are "word messages"? One example is the way we respond to behavior that is unacceptable. Say a little child takes another child's toy and bonks him or her over the head with it. The temptation is to say, "Bad boy! Bad, bad boy!"

The problem is that if this is a pattern of response, eventually the child is going to *believe* the message that he or she is bad. "Mom and Dad keep saying that I'm bad, so I must be a bad person."

Instead, in such situations parents can say something like, "No, no. That is not a good thing to do." The idea is to focus on the *behavior*, not the child. Hitting another child over the head with a toy is what's bad, not the child who does the deed.

It's also important, says Briggs, for parents to reflect children's basic goodness back to them at every opportunity. "Look what a beautiful picture you drew! I like it a lot." "God must love our family very much to have given you to us."

One of the most important skills parents can teach kids today is how to think critically with regard to the media, including television, movies, music, and advertising.

I recall once when one of our sons, then about age six, saw a huge billboard advertising some product or other. "Why do they put up such big signs about stuff like that?" he asked. I explained the basic principle behind much of today's advertising: "Companies put up big signs because the people who make that product want you to want what they have to sell. If they didn't put up such signs you might never want to buy their stuff. That company wants our money, so they try to make us want their product, whether we really want it or not."

This was a basic lesson in relating critically to advertising, and it's the wise parent who takes a similar approach to advertising on television, radio, or via the mail. ("Why do you think the people who make that brand of beer are willing to pay $400,000 per minute to put their advertisements on TV during the Super Bowl?") The same is true for the value messages that are present in just about any movie or television program.

While watching a TV news program, for example, we can say to children, "Who do you think decides what is news and what isn't?" When violence or sex is used in a video movie, "Why do you think the people who made this movie put that in this movie? What does it have to do with the story? I don't think men and women really behave that way toward one another in real life, and I don't think it's good for people to act that way. What do you think?"

One of the best gifts parents can give their children is a sense of discernment. Parents today tend to be especially concerned about their children's sexual attitudes and values. Several studies in recent years have shown, however, that most parents drop the ball when it comes to passing along healthy sexual values. The mass media talk to our kids all the time about them. If parents want their kids to have healthy sexual attitudes they should do some talking as well. Of course, each age level needs a different approach.

When our boys were babies, we gave them lots of physical affection, which told them that their bodies were good. When they were toddlers, we responded honestly to first questions about genitals. During their middle years, we talked openly about puberty, where babies come from, and relating to girls in healthy ways. We have several appropriate books lying around the house that our kids can pick up and leaf through whenever the notion strikes.

Friends who have four kids in their late teens tell us that when it seems natural to do so, they bring up discussions about AIDS at the dinner table and debate the pros and cons of sex outside of marriage. Their kids know that they can ask any question any time. But, says the father in this family, "What we say over and over is that we believe our sexuality is good and a gift of God, and we don't believe it should be abused or treated lightly."

One of the most basic parts of giving kids good sex education at home is also one of the easiest. Carol, a mother of six children, says: "Stephen and I show a lot of physical affection for each other even when the kids are around. We don't get carried away, but we hug and kiss and snuggle. Our kids get the message that Mom and Dad enjoy each other physically, and they also get the message that this sort of thing belongs in marriage."

One of the biggest challenges parents face today is how to deal with the influence of television, videos, movies, and popular music. In this, as in so many aspects of life, parents have more power than they think. There is no law which says that parents must allow their children to watch as much television as they wish; no law that says that the main form of family entertainment must be to watch video movies; and there is no law that says that children should learn to enjoy only popular music.

From the time our three boys were babies, we have played many different kinds of music, from folk to rock, and we have always played a lot of classical music in the evenings.

We are also different in another way. Our kids have always lived in a home with no television. I know that we are not typical, and Kathy and I don't feel that no TV at all is best for everyone. But we are happy with the results.

Our children excel at keeping themselves entertained, they have active imaginations, they do well in school, they enjoy reading, and they have not been exposed to endless television commercials.

In fact, here is something that is perfectly true. To this day, we can walk our boys down the breakfast foods aisle in a supermarket and hear almost nothing about wanting some goofy brand of cereal.

Of course, most parents don't wish to live without television, so we simply advocate strict control. We have friends who set a rule for their kids: no TV on school days, and no more than two hours a day on weekends, holidays, and in the summertime.

Is television a minor issue for parents? I don't think so. In his book, *Magical Child Matures*, Joseph Chilton Pearce, a widely respected authority on child development, says: "Put the child down in front of a television set, the great American baby sitter, and forget about him [or her], as so many of us do. You can also forget about development." The problem, Pearce says, is not with *what* the child watches, but *that* the child watches.

Television floods the imagination with activities that the child should be doing for himself or herself, thus retarding the creativity and the ability to think for oneself. Many educators believe that so-called educational programs for children have little real value. In the words of one authority on education, "*Sesame Street* helps kids do better in school only if school is like *Sesame Street*."

In the early 1970s, the administrative board of the U. S. Catholic Conference published a document that raised another television-related issue. Commercial television, the board said, is doing a much better job indoctrinating people with the idea that happiness comes from shopping than the church is doing at proclaiming the gospel of Jesus.

Sadly, many parents do allow TV to shape their children's most basic values. Why should kids want to go to mass on Sundays when television is so much more captivating?

Neil Postman, a professor of media at New York

University, raises another problem in his book *The Disappearance of Childhood*. He suggests that childhood is becoming a thing of the past because children and adults are watching the same programs on television. For example, it's getting so children know as much about sex and violence as adults do. Parents who strictly limit their children's TV-watching, says Postman, are "performing a noble service."

Now, the point is not that television is the source of all the evils in modern society. In fact, it would be easy to find testimony from other experts that would contradict much of what I have said here about television.

My point is simply this: Parents have a great deal of power to shape their children and they should think twice before turning over that power to an outside influence.

One of the most important ways parents can influence their children is by the kind of environment they build in their home. For example some parents we know decided to encourage quiet in their home. So, each evening at 9:30 they cultivate quiet as a family—no loud music, no noisy appliances, and, yes, no more television. Quiet activities only, please!

When we visit this family, we are always impressed with how calm and quiet the children are compared to many other children. These kids picked up their parents' conviction that building in some quiet time is a healthy thing to do.

In the end, of course, as parents we can only do as much as we can do. The perfect parent does not exist. In the Jewish ceremony called bar mitzvah (for boys) or bat mitzvah (for girls), which celebrates the young person's coming of age, parents say a prayer that goes something like this: "Praise be to you, Lord God, King of the Universe, for I am no longer responsible for my child's behavior."

That's a good prayer for any parent to say once the kids get to a certain age. There comes a time when we must stop feeling responsible for the decisions and choices our offspring make, the good as well as the not-so-good.

Ann Landers was right. One of the best things anyone can do for the world is to raise kids who are able to make the world a better place by how they live their lives. Years ago, Sidney Cornelia Callahan, an author, psychologist, wife and mother of six, put it succinctly. A basic goal of parenting, she said, is "to make our children glad they were born and eager for life."

FAMILY FOCAL POINT 1

One issue that concerns many Catholic parents is how to raise kids so they will want to be Catholics when they grow up. The world gives the church much competition for the hearts and minds of the young. But parents are not without resources. Here are ten tips for raising kids who will want to be good Catholics:

1. Sincerely live your faith in ways that make a difference in your everyday life. Don't be just a Sunday Catholic, but work family prayer—especially table prayer at mealtime that's more than a formality—and active service for others into your life as a family.

2. Develop friendships with other like-minded Catholic families, and spend time with these other families regularly. If you spend time with other families who also require their children to attend mass as a family each Sunday, this becomes less of a point of conflict at home. If our circle of families agrees on basic Christian values, this makes it easier for kids to see the goodness of the faith that we cherish as a family.

3. Make your home more than a secular environment. Display well-done sacred art. See that each bedroom has a crucifix, icon, or picture of the Blessed Mother. Always make the sign of the cross to begin family prayer. Keep Catholic books and magazines in your home, and gear these to all age levels. Read children stories from the lives

of the saints pitched to their age level.

4. Celebrate the liturgical seasons of Advent, Christmas, Lent, and Easter in your home in ways that everyone can see and feel. Put an Advent wreath on or near your family table, and start using an Advent calendar when kids are very young. Read aloud the gospel stories of the birth of Jesus on Christmas eve (Matthew) and Christmas morning (Luke). Make Lent a family observance, with a big feast of a meal the day before Ash Wednesday and receive ashes together as a family. Talk about Easter as the celebration of Jesus' resurrection, and explain that Easter eggs (where baby chicks come from) are a sign of the new life we share in the risen Christ.

5. Take advantage of school or parish religious education programs. Recent studies show that one of the best ways to help kids appreciate their Catholic heritage is to enroll them in Catholic schools. The family is the most important influence on a child, but studies show that kids who attend Catholic schools are much more likely to choose to remain Catholic as adults.

6. Become better informed yourself about your faith. Read at least a couple of good religious books each year. Ask around and you'll soon discover the best books. Parish adult religious education programs can be a great opportunity, too.

7. Talk about our faith at opportune moments when kids are around. Allow religious topics to come up at the dinner table or in the car on family trips, and don't squelch questions or disagreements. With teen-agers, talk about your own struggle to understand and live your faith when you were growing up. With younger children, remark on the signs of God's love in your daily life.

8. Set aside private prayer time each day, and comment on this when kids are present. "An idea came to me during my prayer time today. . ." Share traditional forms of prayer with your children, such as the rosary. Invite

other families to join your family now and then to pray the rosary or to reflect on and pray with scripture, and be sure to include the children.

9. Pray for your children. This sounds obvious, but it's easy to forget that to pray for our children is to entrust them and their lives to God, their Creator.

10. Be patient with your failures as a parent, but do all you can to have a warm, healthy relationship with your children. Martin A. Lang, Ph.D., in his book, *Acquiring Our Image of God*, says: "Fundamentally, affiliation to a religious tradition remains . . . another expression of love for parents."

FAMILY FOCAL POINT 2

What does a good parent do? In her excellent book, *Parenting: The Principles and Politics of Parenthood*, Sidney Cornelia Callahan outlines the basics:

A good parent protects and nurtures the child. By caring for the child the parent "enjoys, entices, and encourages the child into life." But the good parent also "gradually withdraws and separates from the child" so he or she can become more and more independent and mature.

Dr. Callahan cautions parents that, "A shocking amount of parental neglect and lack of protection is creeping into our culture and lifestyles." Under the guise of allowing a child to "be more independent," parents sometimes expose their children to influences today that no child is ready to cope with, such as TV programs and movies that present values that don't fit a Christian perspective.

A good parent also sees to it that the child gets plenty of sleep, nutritious food, and plenty of exercise. "While more people may know more about nutrition than ever before," Dr. Callahan writes, "more children are eating miserably. . . . With affluence and the changing character of food, many children have access to a constant supply of candy, sweets, soda pop, and ice cream as well as a multitude of snack foods."

Finally, Dr. Callahan says, good parents do all they can to make it impossible for their children ever to despair: "they give the basic trust and hope necessary, at the beginning of life."

CHAPTER 7

Single-Parent Families
Are Families Too

SINGLE-PARENT FAMILIES CONSTITUTE a new blip on the Catholic scene, right? Wrong. Single-parent families are a very large "blip" in the life of the church and have been a part of it for many generations. What's different about today is the cause. One hundred years ago, the death of a spouse was the main cause. Today it's mainly divorce, although sometimes women become single parents by deciding to keep, rather than give up for adoption, a baby born out of wedlock.

Christine is thirty years old, she has a boy, eight, and a girl, six, and has been divorced three years. "I work as a legal secretary," she says, "but it took me two years of going to school and leaving my children with my mother to get the training I needed to get this job. It's been a long haul, I can tell you."

Christine is typical of many single mothers in that she does not plan to remain single. "I want my kids to have a family life that includes a dad."

June is in her early forties, has five children ages ten to eighteen, and has been divorced for seven years. "When my husband and I broke up," she says, "I decided that I didn't want to think about getting married again. I have enough to occupy my life with work as a teacher's aid and taking care of my kids. The last thing I want is to get married again."

Most single-parent families are headed by women, but men do sometimes have custody of their children. Mark, who is thirty-two, says, "I live in a world that seems to be filled with single mothers. When my wife left me she simply announced that she didn't want to be a mother anymore, which is sad, I know, but that's the way it is."

Whether a Catholic single-parent family is headed by a mother or father, they tend to share one thing in common. June says it well: "Even today, after seven years, I still feel like we are not a real family."

Whoa! Hold on there! A single-parent family may not fit the traditional model, but it *is* a family. To call such families broken is no help at all. A single-parent family is just that, a *family* with one parent.

Linda, who has three children ages ten, twelve, and fifteen, is an excellent example of a single parent who has high self-esteem, about herself and about her family. "Hey!" she says, grinning. "I've been through the wringer in the last ten years, but I decided very early on that I was a survivor and that my kids and I were going to make the absolute best of a bad deal. And we have. I'm proud of me and I'm proud of us."

How has Linda managed to become such a success story? Basically, it boils down to faith, courage, and refusing to give in to despair. Each single-parent family is unique but Linda tells her story to support groups for divorced Catholics, to college classes, and to counseling groups. Many find new hope from what she has to say.

I joined Linda one day for lunch. For the past three years she has managed a restaurant located in a book store, a job she loves. Linda asks her assistant to keep things under control. As we sit in a corner of the dining area under a huge fern, lively classical music fills the air while people stand chatting in a cafeteria-style line, ordering sandwiches and salads. Linda's shining auburn hair, accented with gray, is pulled back into a bushy pony tail, and she rakes her fingers through it thoughtfully as we talk.

"The first thing I had to overcome," she recalls, "was shame and guilt. I was raised a Catholic and spent twelve years in Catholic schools, and though I value my Catholic education a lot, it also left me with the sense that if there's anything a good Catholic does not do it's get a divorce." Many divorced Catholics know what Linda is talking about. It's not unusual for them to feel left out, ignored, even invisible in their parishes.

"So what I did," Linda explained, "was get some counseling, which I could do for a token fee through Catholic Charities. That helped, just being able to talk with someone about how I was feeling and get some ideas that I could use to cope with my feelings. Then I heard about a support group for divorced Catholic parents, and I joined that. Fortunately, my mom was willing to stay with my kids, and going to weekly meetings was a big help. There I heard the stories of people who were in my position, and I began to realize that this was not the end of the world. My feelings of shame and guilt were not appropriate and were doing nothing but dragging me down."

Linda recalls a retreat she attended that was designed specifically for divorced Catholic parents. The most important part of this retreat was the emphasis it placed on learning again to trust in God's love.

"It was like a revelation," Linda says, smiling. "The retreat master was this priest in his sixties who had done a lot of counseling with divorced Catholics, and he kept repeating some words of Jesus: 'Fear is useless. What is needed is trust' [Mark 5:36]. I tell you, I have never forgotten those words, and they have gotten me through some very hard times."

For Linda, coping with the aftermath of her divorce led to a deeper faith. She developed the habit of saying a short prayer each morning before getting out of bed. She entrusts herself and her children to God for that day, and asks for God's love to surround them all.

Linda also began to realize that she still had a family, therefore they should start acting like a family. "We had a meeting, and I was honest with the kids about my feelings and about my fears," she explains. "But I also asked them to tell me about their feelings and fears, and they did. It was really a good time for us. I said that I wanted us to be a family and to go to mass every Sunday together like a family should, and to say grace together before dinner. Speaking up raised my spirits and the kids said they felt better, too. We hugged and cried a lot that evening."

Another little tradition was born then, too. She recalled hearing someone talk once about giving kids a blessing each night at bedtime. "By-golly, I started doing that every night, and I still do it today, even with my oldest boy, who's fifteen."

Basic to Linda's outlook on life is also plain old gumption. "You have to pray for courage," she says. "You have to pray for the guts to hang in there from one day to the next. I had times when I was unemployed. The older kids got newspaper routes to help us get by. I was on welfare, and my ex-husband was not sending child support money. I really didn't think things could get any worse. I prayed for courage a lot, believe me! And it worked, somehow I had the guts to keep on going, and I still do today."

Are there any particular pitfalls single parents should beware of? "You bet," Linda says. "The most dangerous pitfalls are self-pity and resentment, and what I call the 'super-single-parent syndrome.'

"One of the easiest things in the world for a single parent to do is to give in to self-pity and resentment. Single parents can't get trapped by 'poor, poor me!' and 'I'm going to get even' attitudes. That's asking for nothing but trouble, for themselves and for their kids."

The best way to counteract feelings of self-pity and

resentment? Linda responds, "I'm tempted to say by praying and fasting, which isn't a bad idea. The best way to deal with these feelings is to admit that you feel the way you do, but choose to not act accordingly. Ask for help in prayer. You'd be surprised how hard it is to keep feeling sorry for yourself, and how hard it is to dwell on ways to punish your former spouse when you just try to be with God in love for a few minutes."

The super-single-parent syndrome is the temptation to think that a single parent can be everything two parents can be.

"A single parent is one person, not two. So act like it, already! Stop thinking you can be two parents wrapped up in one. Some things are not going to get done. Kids can help keep the house clean, but it's not going to be as neat and clean as you might like it to be, because you no longer have the time! So what?" Linda believes that meal preparation is more important, as is spending time with your kids. "It's as simple as that."

Frequently, single parents describe themselves as tired. There's no question that terminal fatigue is a genuine hazard of the single-parent's lifestyle. Linda is all over this topic. She leans forward and gently pounds the table with her fist to emphasize the importance of her words.

"Listen, there is absolutely no question that a single parent has a lot of stress. It's no picnic! But that makes taking care of yourself all the more important. A single parent has simply got to make time to take care of herself or himself. Your kids need a parent who more or less has the old act together. You must figure out a way to have some time to yourself on a regular basis."

The great Jewish philosopher, Martin Buber, quoted a traditional rabbinic saying: "A human being who has not a single hour for his [or her] own every day is no human being."

When Linda first learned this lesson, she asked

another single parent if they could trade-off taking care of each other's kids so they each could have one evening a week to go see a movie or play.

"Later, though, I got tired of that and decided that I really wanted one full day each month to go to a retreat house and just be quiet and prayerful all day long. Talk about luxury! So I found someone who wanted the same thing—actually, it's not another single parent, it's a married woman—but her husband's job requires that he travel a lot."

Linda said that she appreciates the chance to have friends who are married, and she tries to bring her family together with two-parent families whenever she can. "We go to every parish potluck and picnic they have."

While she would be the last to say that single-parent families don't have plenty of challenges to face, Linda also bangs the gong for some potential strengths of single-parent families.

"Let's not just look at the negative things. Kids in healthy single-parent families tend to be more mature and more responsible than kids from two-parent families. They have to be, because they have to take up more of the slack around home. Sometimes they also need to get part-time jobs to help out financially. This kind of thing can help a kid to have a sense that, 'Hey, I'm needed by my family and I'm contributing in important ways.'

"Of course, you need to express your appreciation often and be sensitive to possible feelings of self-pity and resentment on the part of your kids, but often kids are glad to be needed in basic ways like this."

Sometimes decision-making can be a major hurdle for single parents, even with regard to everyday matters. Linda recalls one day a few years ago when her daughter was invited to a slumber party. "Wow, you would think this was some really big-deal decision, but I was worried. Was she old enough? I didn't know the family of the girl who had invited her. But she wanted to go in the worst way, so what was I going to do? I mean, I agonized over this!"

Finally, Linda called a friend who was able to help her put the situation in perspective. "That definitely was one of my smarter moves. A single parent should never hesitate to ask for someone else's help even if it seems like an unimportant matter. It can be really hard to make decisions by yourself, especially when it has to do with your kids and what's best for them."

Does Linda have one bit of all-encompassing advice to pass along to other single parents? She takes a sip from her mug of herbal tea and looks up into the fern over our heads for a moment, then she says, "Yeah, I do. Whenever I talk to groups I tell them that no matter what happens, my motto is, 'Don't give up the ship, no matter what.' That may sound trite or superficial, but giving up never did anybody any good; it won't help you and it won't help your kids. Yeah, okay, you've had a hard time of it, but since when did feeling sorry for yourself ever help?"

Most single parents today are divorced. But death still strikes from time to time, and in most respects a single parent who is widowed has just as many difficulties as a divorced single parent.

Bill, whose wife died ten years ago leaving him with eight children ages six to seventeen, identifies with everything that Linda says, including the temptation to indulge in self-pity and resentment, and the temptation to try to be a super-single-parent.

"I struggled with all of that after my wife died," Bill says. "But I must admit that I had one advantage. Whereas a divorced person tends to get these vibes from people that say, 'Oh, you're a bad person,' I got a lot of support. You know, I was the heroic widowed parent, slugging it out through thick and thin."

Bill recalls that one Sunday the gospel reading at mass was from Luke:

> As he drew near to the gate of the city, a man who had died was being carried out, the only son of his mother, and she was a widow.... When the Lord saw her, he was moved with pity for her and said to her, "Do not weep" (7:12-13).

"I'm not kidding," he says, "that hit me right where I lived. From then on, I have always had a deep sense of God's concern for my situation. Here was a story about the compassion of Jesus for a widowed person, just like me. This has been very important for me, and I have read it many, many times late at night when nothing else would help me to keep my head above water."

Bill adds that it is so easy for single parents, whether divorced or widowed, to give up on God's love in their life. "It's easy for us to think that we have to do it all alone. Yet even when we don't get the support from our parish that we'd like to have, we are never alone. Never. The caring and powerful love of God is there, and in our family we have been given to one another as signs of love by a loving God. I really believe that Christ extends his hand to single parents every day and says, 'Trust me, I am worthy of trust.' And it's true. I've always found it to be so."

FAMILY FOCAL POINT 1

Support groups for separated and divorced Catholics are fairly common today. Usually they help with the transition for those whose marriages have ended in the past couple of years. They offer opportunities to gather for social purposes, but more importantly, they present a chance for shared prayer, group retreats, and special liturgies.

One of the most important forms of therapy a newly separated or divorced person needs is someone who has gone through the same experience and can be a sympathetic listener. Support groups for separated and divorced Catholics provide a forum for such healing to happen.

Martha, who was divorced three years ago, comments: "Right after my ex-husband and I split up, I was at wit's end. I was an emotional basket case. Then I read in the parish bulletin about a support group for separated and divorced Catholics, and I decided to go. That was the hardest thing I've ever had to do, because it meant I had to admit to myself and other people that I was divorced. I was really nervous, but by the time the evening was over, I felt better. Even that early in my divorce I began to think that maybe there was a light at the end of the tunnel."

Julio, divorced for two years, agrees: "One of the toughest things I had to deal with was the feeling that because I was divorced I was a bad person and a bad Catholic. Joining a support group helped me to get over that kind of thing. It really was a big help."

FAMILY FOCAL POINT 2

Gordon, who is divorced and a single parent, calls for more sensitivity to single parents as potential leaders:

"Someone needs to speak up for the needs of single-parent families in our parishes, and who better than a single parent? Such a person can say, 'I've paid my dues as a single parent.' Such a person knows what it feels like to experience a divorce as a Catholic, or to have a loved spouse die. He or she has coped with the financial worries, the sexual frustrations, and the spiritual desert unique to the experience of divorce or being widowed and trying to raise kids without the help of a partner.

"Often we miss the other side of these experiences, which is a growth in compassion for all who suffer and more freedom to rejoice with those who rejoice. The single parent, through his or her experiences, often becomes a deeper, more mature person, and such a person is a prime candidate for lay ministry in a parish."

CHAPTER 8

How to Have a Family You Can Feel Good About

YOU KNOW THE OLD BIT ABOUT HOW to tell a pessimist from an optimist: hand the person a partially filled glass of water. An optimist will say it's half-full, a pessimist will say half-empty. And more often than not you'll find yourself in the presence of a pessimist. We tend to see what's not there rather than what is there.

The same is often true of families. We tend to see our family's weak spots, the things we don't like, and pass by the strong points. What's needed is a change of perspective. It's easy to see that the glass is half-full and that most of us have healthier families than we think we do.

"I don't feel so great about my family," a young woman said during a break in a workshop on family spirituality. "It seems like the baby is always fussy, we're always tired from the treadmill of work, and the older kids don't care whether they get their homework done or not. And we fight a lot, too. It seems like we hardly ever just enjoy one another like I always thought a family should."

I asked this woman to sit down with a pencil and a sheet of paper and write down ten good things that had happened in her family in the last two weeks. I asked her to be very specific and to leave out all negative observations. "O.K.," she said, "but it's not going to be easy."

A few minutes later, smiling, she handed me her paper. "Here," she said. "Thanks for asking me to do that.

I guess things aren't as bad as I thought."

Here is what this young woman wrote:

1. My husband and I said we loved each other almost every day.

2. We did not go without food, clothing, and shelter.

3. Twice we popped popcorn and played a game together as a family.

4. We said grace before every evening meal.

5. We worked out a way to share the household chores more evenly.

6. We went to mass together both Sundays.

7. One evening my oldest son gave me a hug and said thanks for the special dinner (and I almost fainted).

8. One evening my husband and I got a sitter and went out for dinner and a movie.

9. After we had a talk with her, our second oldest daughter has been a lot better about not fighting with her younger brother.

10. One day my husband and I did something "terrible." We both called in sick, stayed home, got the older kids off to school, puttered around the house all day, and made love while the baby was taking her nap.

Most of us, if we stop to think about it, find that we can say similar things about our own families, too. Family life will never be hassle-free, but we need to recognize that the glass is more than half-full and our families are more than half-healthy. Give yourself a pat on the back. You deserve it!

It also is true that most of us would like to have families that are happier and healthier. So the rest of this chapter will focus on ways to make a basically good thing better.

A few years ago, Catholic family-life author and speaker Dolores Curran decided to ask a few hundred people how they would describe a healthy family. So she submitted a series of questions to professionals who work with families. Counselors and therapists, teachers, doctors, religious leaders, social workers, nurses, scout leaders, and a raft of other people replied. In fact, she mailed out 500 questionnaires and got 551 back! One family therapist thought what Curran was doing was so important she made her own extra copies and asked fifty-one of her fellow professionals to fill them out.

She reported her findings in the book *Traits of a Healthy Family.* "Thousands of families," Curran says, "are making the world go on in positive and hopeful ways today. . . . Let others proclaim the death of the family, not I nor my colleagues who work with such families."

Curran concluded from her survey that healthy families tend to have fifteen traits or characteristics. What follows is a list of the traits I judge to be the most important and examples of ways we can use them as guidelines to nourish our own ordinary families.

The healthy family communicates and listens.

Brace yourself. Did you know that according to studies done since the 1970s, in the average American family husbands and wives spend only a few minutes a week talking about anything important? The same is true of parent-child relationships: most parents and kids spend very little time talking about any but the most superficial topics.

"I believe it," says Marta, a young mother. "Look at our family's schedule. Our calendar looks like a disaster area!"

But let's back up for just a second here. Why is it important for families to communicate and listen? The answer isn't hard to find. The main purpose of family life is creating and sustaining loving relationships, and that's why communication and listening is so important.

If loving relationships are what family life is for, communication and listening is how we love. Little time spent talking about the things we feel most deeply, plus little time spent really listening to one another, equals relationships that are less loving than they could be. It's as simple as that.

Mike and Mary Ann have been married ten years and have four young children. He explains that a time came when they decided to put the family on their calendar along with all the demands on their time and energy. "We just decided," Mike recalls, "that *we* are at least as important as work and outside meetings, so *we* deserve time, too."

For example, they scheduled a weekly family night. Now, each Sunday evening the family gathers, turns off the TV, and they talk, address complaints family members have, and play a game. Then, they light a candle and turn off all the lights and give each person a chance to express some informal prayer.

"The first few times we did this," Mary Ann says, "I had tears in my eyes by the time it was over. I didn't realize how mature our kids are spiritually, they really are wonderful."

The healthy family fosters table time and conversation.

Actually, Mike and Mary Ann's decision to have a weekly family night was the *second* way they chose to cultivate regular communication and listening. The *first* way was to place a high priority on everyone being present for their evening meal.

"We decided that this is critical," Mike says. "All these outside voices demand we be someplace else when we should be home together around our table. Employers want us to work more overtime, school sports programs want kids to spend hours practicing after school, various groups want us to attend meetings. Baloney! We just decided to take back control of our time and say, 'We come first.'"

The point is not that all families must have every evening meal together, of course. But nothing but good can come from the decision to have everyone regularly present for family meals even if it's only two or three times a week.

One reason the family meal is so important is that we are never more a family than when we gather to break bread together. "We find this to be true," Mary Ann says. "Of course, our family meal is never something out of a Norman Rockwell painting. It's rather chaotic. But all the same, when we sit down we share more than food. We share what fills our hearts and we nourish one another that way. Even if a meal erupts in conflict we at least are relating to one another, and that's what's important."

The healthy family has a shared religious core.

Carl and Jeanette discovered the importance of this several years ago when, after their first baby was born, they had to sit down and talk about their baby's baptism. "It was kind of spooky," Jeanette says. "We realized that we should have talked about this stuff before we got married, but like your typical engaged couple, flying high, we didn't think it was important. After all, we were both Catholic."

Finally, after much talking and some tears, they realized they both had underestimated the importance of a shared family faith. "Something about having a baby," Carl says, "impressed on us the fact that we could never hope to raise children and keep our marriage together without God's help. So we started going to mass every Sunday, and we got to know some more experienced parents in our parish who helped us to see how important it is to make our family a little Christian community."

Carl and Jeanette trace their religious concerns to the fact that when they talked about having their baby baptized, they realized they did not want to raise a child who would have no way to escape self-centeredness. "We live in a world that encourages selfishness," Jeanette says, "and we don't agree with that. Our shared faith as a family is a source of support when the going gets rough. But it also helps to focus on God in our midst and on God's call to help one another and people outside our family who need our help."

Before long, these new parents also learned the importance of shared family traditions—both religious and non-religious—such as shared prayer around the table, having an Advent wreath, and picnics in a park during the summer months.

The healthy family values service to others.

When Tim and Alice were engaged they attended a special weekend program for engaged couples. Several veteran married couples shared personal experiences of the ups and downs of marriage and responded to questions from the engaged couples. The married couples encouraged the future spouses to get involved in serving others as a way to nourish their own marriages.

At the end of the weekend, the married couples invited the engaged couples to give them a call after they had been married for a year or two and volunteer to help with this same program. Tim and Alice decided that they liked this idea, and they did call after they had been married for a year.

"There is something very special," Alice says, "about joining a group effort that is geared to helping others at a special time in their life. Tim and I wouldn't give up doing this kind of thing for all the tea in China. Also, it's a great experience for our twins to join us when we help give this program. They're little now, but still they see that mom and dad value serving others, and we hope that they will want to do the same."

Families find many ways to help others. Those who do become convinced that it is one of the best ways to help their own family stay healthy. Families help out with hot meal programs for the poor, take in foster children, and decide together which good cause will get their monthly tithe.

Dick and Germaine and their two teen-age daughters decided years ago to adopt a family in a country in Central America. Through a program in their diocese, they give money each month to help a family become self-sufficient.

"It really turned out to be a great thing for us," Dick says. "We got so involved that last year we saved up and visited the first family we were matched with. It was a great experience for all of us, and our girls saw firsthand the contrasts between how we live and how most of the rest of the people in the world live. You just can't buy that kind of education."

The healthy family admits to and seeks help with problems.

Can it be? A healthy family has problems? Yes, indeed. A major difference between a healthy family and one that is less than healthy is that the healthy family admits it has a problem and looks it in the eye.

A family that is *not* healthy will play all kinds of psychological games to avoid facing up to its problems. Such a family is a victim of the perfect family syndrome. It thinks that a problem is something to be ashamed of, that a healthy family should never have any problems. But nothing could be further from the truth.

The main way that ordinary healthy families deal with problems is to develop problem-solving techniques. Above all, it learns to negotiate. "We learned this lesson well," says the father of four teen-agers. "When we see that two or more of us are going for the jugular, we know it's time to talk and time for everyone concerned to be ready to compromise."

It's important to realize that there's a difference between a difficulty and a problem. When a kid has trouble in school, either with studies or with relationships with other kids, this is a difficulty. A problem is something that, after all the family's best efforts, does not go away. A teen-ager who is depressed to the point of being suicidal is a problem. A parent who drinks too much is a problem. "Actually," says a family therapist, "each family has to learn to tell a problem from a difficulty, but generally families are naturally pretty good at this. They can trust their own instincts."

A problem may require professional help and/or the help of a support group such as Alcoholics Anonymous, Al-Anon (for families of alcoholics) or Alateen.

We need to look at a family member's problem as something that concerns the whole family. In a very real sense, each family member contributes to and suffers from, for example, one member's alcoholism. When one member of a family has a problem, the whole family has a problem.

The main points are these: A healthy family is not surprised when difficulties and problems develop, and it learns problem-solving skills and seeks professional help when it's needed.

The healthy family has a sense of play and humor.

"I'll tell you what works best for our family when it comes to both getting things done and enjoying the everyday business of just living together. We kid around a lot, that's what."

The speaker is a single mother in her mid-forties who has four teen-age children. "You know how we have some of our best times? In the evening, when we are all together for dinner, someone will make a terrible pun, then someone else will pick it up and make another pun, and pretty soon we're groaning and laughing. We really have become expert punners."

Another parent, a father of two boys ages eight and ten, explains that his family enjoys going to baseball games together. "That's something I value a great deal," he says. "It gives us a chance to let our hair down and just have fun together."

Clearly, a family benefits from being able to laugh and play together. One mother says that she even uses a lighthearted approach to getting kids to do as they are asked. "When I want a kid to do his or her housecleaning job, for example, often I sing it instead of saying it. I adopt this kind of crazy opera-singer voice and sing, 'Please, oh, please, come down and vacuum the living rooooom. La-la-la-la!' This doesn't always work, but it helps to side step a fight over getting the house cleaned."

There is something very healthy about a family where kidding around, joking, and playing punctuates the family's day-in day-out existence.

It's odd, when you think about it. To have a family we can feel good about takes work. We have to go to the trouble to communicate and listen, share meals together, share our faith, serve one another and others who have special needs, expect and face up to difficulties and problems, and make the effort to laugh and play.

"Yeah, it takes work," says one father, "but I challenge anyone to find anything more worth working for."

FAMILY FOCAL POINT 1

Unfortunately, families—especially those with young children—often find it difficult to be together in church. Here are some tips on how to be together in ways that will nourish family affection, rather than build up more stress:

- *Snuggle and hug.* The eucharist is not the time for private devotions. It is meant to be a communal *activity.* (Remember, at the Last Supper, Jesus said, "Do this . . . ," he didn't say, "Pray about this," or "Meditate on this," or "Think about this.") So we find that during mass is a great time to hold kids on your lap, give hugs, and snuggle. This is a great way to associate feelings of being loved with being in church.

- *Sing "la la la."* Young children find it tough to be quiet in church, so during times when everyone else is speaking or singing, encourage your child to make sounds, too. When the congregation sings, encourage "la la la," even if the child can't carry a tune in a bucket. This makes it easier for a kid to be quiet when it's time to be quiet again.

- *Play find the number.* Find a page or hymn number in a song book, and ask the child to see how fast she or he can find that number. This can go on indefinitely, and you can do it and still pay attention to the liturgy.

- Use a logical consequence to help children learn—as they get older—to choose appropriate behavior in church. Gear the quality of behavior to donuts after mass. Excellent behavior rates a frosted donut; so-so behavior gets a plain cake donut; and completely unacceptable behavior means no donut at all. Remember on this one to always be consistent. Don't say one thing and do another.

FAMILY FOCAL POINT 2

In their excellent book, *What to Do After You Turn Off the TV*, Frances Moore Lappe and Family offer suggestions for ways families can make ordinary times around home more enjoyable.

During the evening meal—after your family has finished table prayer—each person gets a chance to tell the best and worst things that happened that day. This is a great way to find out about family members' feelings, what they are worried about or what they are happy about. Information surfaces about events at school or work that might not come out at all. Also, children begin to under-stand that mom and dad have their highs and lows, too, and they become comfortable with the idea of sharing feelings and concerns.

Make housecleaning less stressful! Have a meeting on a weekly or monthly basis, and divide up the chores. (It's fair to rotate these so everyone gets all the jobs sooner or later.) Turn on some music. Families find it helpful sometimes when everyone agrees to sing "Whistle While You Work." Or make cleaning into an adventure by naming various areas: the kitchen is the dungeon, the hallway is a tunnel full of ferocious alligators, mom's and dad's room is the chamber of the king and queen. And so forth.

When all the cleaning is finished, reward yourselves. Go out to an inexpensive restaurant for a late breakfast or lunch, visit the zoo, or go ice-skating. And then come home to a clean house!

At our house, we decided that life without a dish-washing machine has its advantages. When one parent and one kid wash the dishes together at the end of the day, plenty of good talk happens, too.

CHAPTER 9

Families Are Called to Service

WHAT GIVES A CHRISTIAN FAMILY its unique identity and character? One thing we can focus on is the fact that a Christian family is called to reach out to others in service and prayer. Just as Jesus in the Last Supper narrative in John's gospel washed his disciples' feet, Christians are called to serve and care for one another within the family. But a Christian family is called to do more, to live with a view to the whole world.

Parents have a special responsibility to help their children see that what happens in their family affects the wider community. For example, what a family decides to do with its empty aluminum soda pop cans has an effect on the quality of life in the wider environment. So, let's recycle!

The idea is not to make wild-eyed radicals out of our family members, but to remember that everything we do affects others. For example, millions of people are hungry in the world, and they are our brothers and sisters. As a family, we can support such organizations as Bread for the World, which works to overcome hunger.

Leo and Marge have been married for fifteen years, and have a ten-year-old boy and an eight-year-old girl. Leo works for an architectural firm as a draftsman. Marge is a legal secretary.

Stan, a computer programmer, is a divorced single

father whose three teen-age children live with their mother in another city.

Bill and Clara have been married for forty years and are now retired, their five children long gone to lives of their own. However, the youngest, a woman of twenty-eight, and her four-year-old son, are now living with Bill and Clara after a recent divorce.

Finally, there's Carol Ann, twenty-six, who became a single mother six years ago and now works as a secretary for an appliance repair company. She has an apartment of her own and her mother takes care of her daughter after school until Carol Ann gets off work.

These families all have different lives, but they also have something in common. They give about one evening each month to help out with a hot meal program for the poor. They do this not because they think of themselves as super-Christians or because they're trying to impress someone, but because they realize that their lives are more complete, somehow more worth living, when they share their lives and resources with others.

Carol Ann, the young single mother, collects her daughter from her mother's place on the second Thursday of each month, then drives to the inner city parish where the hot meal program operates.

"I'm always tired after a day at work," Carol Ann remarks. "But this is something I have to do. I really need to be there, not just to 'do good unto' some people who are less fortunate than I am, but to receive from them, too. I get more from serving them than they get from me, I think. I still feel tired later. But when I get home I always feel better than I did before. I think it's good for my daughter, too, to be in that situation. She's learning what it means to give and to share."

One of the best-known stories in the New Testament (Matthew 25:31-46) sheds much light on why families find it important to get involved with and share their love with others outside their immediate family.

Jesus says that when "the Son of Man comes in his glory, and all the angels with him, he will sit upon his glorious throne, and all the nations will be assembled before him." And God will divide people into two groups, "as a shepherd separates the sheep from the goats," the sheep on his right, the goats on his left.

The sheep, on God's right, will "inherit the kingdom," while the goats, on the left, will get "eternal fire." And the only difference between the two groups in this story is that the first group gave food and drink to those who needed it and clothing to those who had none. They cared for those who were sick and visited those in prison, and the other group did not.

In Jesus' story, he identifies himself with those who are hungry, without clothing, and so forth. Jesus says that to care for those with special needs, "these least brothers of mine," is to care for him, and "what you did not do for one of these least ones, you did not do for me."

Before we go any further it's important to make one point; charity still begins at home. "We wouldn't miss our involvement each month in the hot meal program," says Leo, "but at the same time we realize that the most basic forms of service for Marge and me still happen in the context of our own family. The ways we care for one another and for our children on a day-in, day-out basis are real ways to serve others, too."

Indeed, parents often need to appreciate that in feeding and clothing their children they do it for Jesus himself. Every day, family members feed the hungry, clothe the naked, care for those who are ill, and comfort the lonely within their own families. When these things go on in a family the spirit of the gospel is very much alive.

Stan, the divorced father mentioned earlier, considers it one of the most important things he can do for his teen-age kids to write each of them a letter once a week.

"Usually, I do this on Sunday afternoons, after I've been to mass. I write about things that have been going on for me during the previous week, and I ask about things that I know have been going on for each of my kids. I also talk about people I meet at the hot meal program and about that whole situation.

"I think it helps my kids to see that there's more to life than high school. It's easy for teen-age kids to get too wrapped up in themselves. Of course, when my kids visit me, I bring them along to the meal program so they have some firsthand experience of what I'm talking about."

The point is that one of the most important things a Christian family can do for itself is to forget about its own concerns and worries in order to reach out to others who have special needs. This takes different forms for different families, of course.

The Corrigan family, Pete, Lynn, and their four children, ages four through thirteen, discovered a few years ago that they wanted to do something for others as a family, but they didn't know exactly what. "We had a family meeting," Pete recalls, "and we decided that for the next couple of weeks we would do some thinking about it, and the older kids volunteered to do some research. Then at our next meeting we would see what ideas we had for serving others together."

There were no end of possibilities, but the one they decided to try first ended up being the one with which they stayed. The Corrigans are now a foster family. Lynn is a full-time homemaker, which makes it easier for them to do this, but the whole family gets involved.

"I wasn't too crazy about the idea of sharing my room with some strange kid," says Kevin, age nine. "But I agreed to try it out, and it hasn't been too bad most of the time."

The Corrigans find that sharing their life as a family with kids who come from unhealthy family situations helps them as much as it does the foster children.

"Our kids learned quickly," says Pete, "that a lot of the things they thought were so important—new clothes, a late model car, stereo sets—aren't nearly as important as having a family that loves you. Some of the stories they heard from foster kids have helped them be more compassionate and less selfish. Of course, there are plenty of tough times with foster kids around, so we have had to learn to deal with conflict and resentment, and I think that has helped our kids to become more mature as individuals."

It's especially beneficial for families to get involved in serving others *together*. In fact, it can be risky for family members to get too heavily involved in good causes as individuals. A good example comes from Charles Dickens' famous novel *Bleak House*.

In this wonderful story, Dickens painted a portrait of a character called Mrs. Jellyby, who is forever working to improve the lives of "the natives of Borrioboola-Gha, on the left bank of the Niger." The trouble is, she neglected her own children. They are poorly fed, dirty, and ill-clad, and her husband has become sullen and withdrawn.

Mrs. Jellyby is the classic do-gooder whose many works of charity cause her own family to suffer. Her story shows what can easily happen if parents become so involved in helping others that they spend less and less time with their own children. It's good for married couples, for example, to care enough to serve in programs designed to help other married couples have better marriages. But it's not good if they become so enthusiastic about this that they don't spend enough time with their own family.

In fact, one of the best ways to plant the seeds of resentment in the hearts of children, with regard to the church, is to use church-related activities as an excuse for neglecting children or family life in general. A form of service to others is good only if it benefits the family as a whole. Remember, the most important form of church life for families is family life.

Hans and Mallene, whose four children are now grown and gone, recall how important this consideration was for them when they first decided to get involved in service as a family.

"When our kids were still young, we helped out with a youth group in our parish," Hans recalls. "We looked for service projects for the youth group to help out with. We painted a couple of houses for older people, that sort of thing. But we always brought our own kids along to help out, even though they didn't really help much. At least that made this a family activity, not just something mom and dad were doing."

A few years later, a priest invited this couple to help give a program for engaged couples, to help them prepare for marriage. "We accepted," Mallene says. "But we insisted that our kids be able to come along, too."

What started out as a Sunday afternoon program soon grew into a weekend-long program, and before long Hans and Mallene were helping give the program about one weekend each month. "It became a very important thing for our family," Hans says. "Our kids would help set up chairs, show the engaged people to their rooms, and generally be around during the weekend. Just by being there they helped the engaged couples to get a more family oriented perspective on marriage. Of course, they saw mom and dad doing this and they learned, I think, the value of serving others."

A family regularly serving others together has a positive impact on both parents and children. Indeed, involvement in serving others alongside their parents is one of the best forms of "religious education" children can receive. This way, kids learn from experience that faith is a way of life, that a Christian commitment should make a real difference in the ways we choose to use the time of our life.

Don, a young father, adds another important insight. "One of the big problems kids seem to have with their parents' religion," he says, "is when faith seems to be hypocritical. I think that when a family gets involved in various service activities, it shows kids that religion is not just a Sunday-only matter. This makes it almost impossible for kids to call their parents hypocrites and nothing more than Sunday Catholics."

I don't wish to suggest, of course, that a Catholic family should do its best to be a miniature St. Vincent dePaul Society. Now and then families do "go the extra mile" and embrace the voluntary simplicity of life needed to join a Catholic Worker house of hospitality, for example. Other families join Maryknoll or another overseas missionary society for a few years. But most families integrate the need to serve others into their ordinary day-to-day life.

Sometimes families get involved in service in ways that are so informal that they themselves hardly notice what they're doing. Richard and Mary happen to own a small lake cabin, and for many years they have encouraged friends to use their cabin whenever they themselves are not using it.

"This doesn't sound like much," Richard says. "But families benefit a lot from being able to have a weekend at the lake. This dawned on us not long ago. Our society does not encourage this kind of sharing, so we try to do it as much as we can."

The examples of ways families can serve others are almost endless. Mike and Nancy, a young couple with no children of their own as yet, spend one Saturday a month driving around collecting baby supplies for redistribution by a pregnancy care agency. "This gives us a chance," Nancy says, "to resist the self-centeredness that our society encourages in young couples like us. It helps us to think about someone besides ourselves and our tendency to want to do little more than become as comfortable as possible."

Often, people in families think that the first thing they

need to do to become more Christian is to make more time for family prayer, or perhaps more time to read and discuss the Bible together. These things are good, of course, but I would say that the first step to becoming a more Christian family is to look for a way to serve others together. Indeed, a dedication to family prayer goes hand-in-hand with a dedication to serving others. The two just naturally go together.

FAMILY FOCAL POINT 1

The Second Vatican Council pointed out that God gives the family the mission of being the primary vital cell of society. To accomplish this mission the Council encouraged the mutual affection of family members, family prayer, understanding of the family as the home church, participating in liturgical worship, offering hospitality, and helping provide for those in need.

> Among the various works of the family apostolate the following may be listed: adopting abandoned children, showing a loving welcome to strangers, helping with the running of schools, supporting adolescents with advice and help, assisting engaged couples to make a better preparation for marriage, taking a share in catechism-teaching, supporting married people and families in a material or moral crisis, and in the case of the aged not only providing them with what is indispensable but also procuring for them a fair share of the fruits of economic progress.
>
> —Decree on the Apostolate of the Laity, #11

FAMILY FOCAL POINT 2

> The Christian family has a mission to the world and must avoid the temptation to turn inward upon itself. It must have a commitment outside and beyond itself, greater even than its concern for its own survival. A family whose basic goals and lifestyle are focused inward for its own enjoyment

or preservation is like a pond. A pond may become stagnant and even dry up if there are no fresh sources of water flowing into it nor any outlets for water to flow through it. A family in mission, one that lives for the world, is like a river or a stream. Fresh water from its source flows through it to carry refreshment and new life downstream as it flows onward and outward to the sea.

—from *Christians in Families*, by Ross T. Bender

CHAPTER 10

Family Prayer
and Ritual

REMEMBER THAT WONDERFUL SCENE in *Fiddler on the Roof,* when the Jewish peasant Tevye and his wife Golda gather their family around the table to celebrate the beginning of Sabbath? It is a moment often recalled as one of the warmest and most touching in this delightful musical. Golda lights the Sabbath candles as she and Tevye together sing:

May the Lord protect and defend you.

May He always shield you from shame . . .

Why do you suppose this scene brings a tear to the eye? It may have something to do with our longing today for ways to ritualize our feelings for one another within our families. We crave ways to pray together such as Tevye and Golda have, ways that will touch us deeply and bring us closer together.

The good news is that family prayer and ritual are not as difficult as we may suspect. Before I go any further, however, I want to put family prayer and ritual in their proper place. I purposely left this topic for last because sometimes we think that the first and most important thing to do if we want to have a healthier, more Christian family is to start praying together frequently. But I don't believe that for a minute.

The first and most important step a family can take to nourish and enrich its life in the fullest and most human sense is to set aside time to be together as a family. For relating to God, so to speak, doesn't click unless we are also relating to people. In other words, our relationship with God hinges on our family relationships.

As I indicated earlier, married couples need time together on a regular basis away from the kids. Single parents need time to themselves. And parents and children need frequent opportunities simply to be together, to talk and enjoy one another. In this context, family prayer begins to make sense.

Mark and Judy, who have four children, recall their own experience: "We attended an enrichment evening for parents in our parish a couple of years ago," Mark recalls, "and we came away with the conviction that we needed to work regular time together into our life as a couple and as a family. We started having a family night every other week, and an evening out every other week for Judy and me, and praying together became easier. It started feeling like something we really wanted and needed to do."

But that's not all. As we also saw earlier, families need a chance once a month or so to share themselves with those who have special needs. We families tend to have a desperate need to get out of ourselves by serving others. We spend so much time worrying about ourselves, about our needs and desires, about our problems and our kids' problems, that it's easy to turn in on ourselves. Often we don't realize that many of our problems would seem much smaller, or might even disappear, if we would forget about ourselves and our problems long enough to care occasionally about someone else's problems.

Judy explains that this was exactly the experience she and Mark and their children had: "It was good for us to spend time as a couple and as a family, but after a few weeks of this we began to feel like professional navel-gazers. A single parent in our parish told us about a small community for mentally handicapped adults with whom she and her kids had gotten involved, so we went along one Saturday afternoon and we've been helping out there about once a month ever since."

And that, Mark adds, seemed to be just what their family needed. "It's like we were out of balance as a family, and getting involved with this community gave us the balance we needed. This has been especially good for our kids. It has helped them experience what it feels like to forget themselves now and then and focus on somebody else's needs. And the interesting thing is that this has enriched our family prayer a lot. Now, when we pray around our dinner table, we think about more than our own needs and troubles."

Family time together, family involvement with those who have some special needs, and family prayer and rituals: this is the ideal balance for any family.

Now that we understand the need to view family prayer and ritual as part of a bigger picture, we can offer some ideas on how families can pray and celebrate rituals together.

The first principle to keep in mind when your family gathers to discuss ways to pray is that family prayer is not something you do to make your family holy. Your family is *already* holy (remember: hale and hearty). A family prays together to recognize and celebrate the holiness that's there but we are often too busy to see.

Here's an example of what I mean. When our three boys were still quite young, about ages two to six, all three received new and/or used riding toys: a bike, a tricycle, and a little straddle-and-push-with-your-feet contraption. Out of the blue, we recognized that this was not just an ordinary event for our kids, this was a sacred moment.

We wanted to help our boys realize that the joy they felt riding their new toys was an everyday experience of God, so I quickly got a candle while Kathy gathered all three on the sidewalk in our front yard. We handed the lighted candle to each one in turn (fortunately there was no wind!) and as we did so we said a short impromptu blessing: "May God bless you and keep you safe and give you much joy in your play on this new toy."

Well, these three ordinary boys couldn't have been more thrilled. Off they wheeled, and our little spontaneous family ritual had made even more special an already delightful moment.

We have found it good to be ready with this kind of simple ritual spontaneity. It helps children and parents alike to be more sensitive to the holy in the ordinary.

A friend of ours who is the father of two teen-agers put it this way: "The world is constantly telling our kids that time is money and don't believe in anything you can't lay your hands on. Spontaneous family rituals tell kids that time is God's gift of life, and that God's love is all around, no matter what else is going on."

We can't expect to be spontaneous all the time, of course. As a family, we need to schedule regular times when we pray together whether we feel spontaneous or not. And the best time for this is at mealtime. Earlier, we talked about how important the family meal is. One reason is that it offers a natural time for family prayer.

"So a family never prays together at any other time except before their evening meal," said Monica, a mother of two pre-teen girls and a boy. "That's just fine. That, all by itself, is great, and a family should feel good about it."

See, a family's main meal is loaded with sacred meaning. Sure, if children are involved, mealtime is likely to be chaotic. But that's O.K. For mealtime is also an opportunity to bless one another and the food we are about to share, and that's a very big deal.

Monica comments: "We do a lot more than eat when we sit down around the table to share a meal as a family. We come to the table with not only a hunger for food. We come with a need to give and receive emotional and spiritual nourishment, too."

How can our family make mealtime more prayerful? Some of the ways we can do this are the very picture of simplicity, but they make a wonderful difference.

We recommend a tradition that has been a part of our family's life since before our children were born. Each evening before our meal prayer we light a candle in the middle of our table. This doesn't sound like much, but believe me it is a powerful symbol.

In the course of our children's younger years, each one asked: "Why do we have a candle here, anyway?" Talk about an opening! "We light a candle during dinner to remind us that Jesus is with us when we gather around our table to share a meal. We do this because Jesus said that we are the light of the world, and we want to remember that."

We take turns allowing each family member to decide exactly what our table prayer will be. Some like to begin with the refrain from a song, followed by a spoken prayer from each of us. Others prefer silent prayer as we hold hands around the macaroni and cheese. During special seasons, such as Advent and Lent, we begin each meal with the same song. During Advent, for example, it's "O Come, O Come, Emmanuel."

It's important to watch for moments that are already important and meaningful, then think of a way to whistle up the loving God who dwells therein.

Another important moment for kids is bedtime. The darkness is about to descend at the end of another day that has been loaded with God's gifts.

Parents have all kinds of ways to make the goodnight moment special. Marta, a single mother, explains her approach: "My daughter is four years old, and I sing a song. 'Swing Low, Sweet Chariot' seems to have all kinds of wonderful images for a child. Then I help my daughter say a little nighttime prayer, and I end by placing my hand on her head while I say, 'God bless you.'"

The idea of giving children a parental blessing is one which seems to be catching on. As parents, we can give our children a blessing no one else can give them. My approach at bedtime is to trace a little sign of the cross on the child's forehead with my thumb while I say, "God be with you all through the night."

Special events that touch the whole family are ideal times for prayer and ritual, too. When Marta bought a new car, she and her daughter said a little blessing over some water, then took it out and sprinkled it on the new car. Marta said an informal prayer asking God to bless the car and help them to be safe while riding in it, then she helped her daughter to sprinkle some more of the blessed water on the car.

"It really wasn't a big deal," Marta says, "but it was kind of neat. A car is an important part of our life and we tend to spend a lot of time in it, so why not remind ourselves that even in our car God's love goes with us?"

Mike and Carolyn, who have four teen-age children, explain that they have had to be adaptable when it comes to family prayer times. "When our kids were little," Mike says, "we could do things that worked with little kids. Now that they're teen-agers, we find that the best approach, apart from grace before meals, is to have everybody set aside an evening every two or three weeks when we will all be home. About nine o'clock, when homework is basically done, or people can take a break, we gather in the living room. Then we darken the room and light a candle in the middle of the room. We sit on the couch, or stretch out on the floor, or whatever each one wants to do.

"And then, actually, we don't do much. I usually say a little prayer where I talk about how we're all tired and busy and so forth, and I ask God to be with us now, or something like that. Then we just spend the next half-hour or so being there together in the dark around the lighted candle. And if someone wants to say something, or say a prayer, that's fine. We all listen. Sometimes good stuff comes out about things going on in our individual lives, now and then we laugh, and once in a while there are tears.

"Then, when we all feel like it's over, we join hands in a circle and quietly say the Our Father. Most times we end with hugs all around, too. And that's about it."

It's also easy to integrate the Bible into family life. Some families make a special place to display it in their homes, and they use scripture as part of their family table prayer. We found that as our boys got to the age where they could read, they enjoyed an illustrated version called *The Picture Bible*. This was a natural lead-in to reading a real Bible later.

Sometimes young Catholics find fundamentalist churches attractive because they emphasize the Bible. More often than not, these are young people who grew up in Catholic families where scripture was not a part of ordinary life. Wise parents let their kids see them reading the Bible and they incorporate scripture into family prayer, even in the simplest of ways.

Families pray together in so many different ways. A family I visited said what struck me as a rather long collection of formal prayers after dinner. But the feeling was good and the love around the table was obvious.

An ordinary family event, the celebration of a birthday, is also a sacred event. We're celebrating God's creation of a completely unique person, a member of our family, an intimate companion in life. Yet often Catholic families fail to allow birthdays to be holy events. We light candles on a cake, sing "Happy Birthday," and pass around the presents. What a shame! All it takes is adding a prayer to the ritual to glimpse its sacred character.

Special seasons of the year, especially Advent, Christmas, Lent, and Easter, bring many opportunities for special family rituals. No Catholic home should be without an Advent wreath in the weeks before Christmas. Many families with older children find that if you do something two years in a row it's a tradition.

Finally, I'd like to suggest one other dimension to family prayer that has enriched our lives.

A few years ago, we called on several other parents who are friends and asked if they would like to get together one evening a month, without children, for prayer and conversation. About ten jumped at the opportunity. So, usually on the first Friday of each month, we gather in the home of one family or another. We chat and catch up on one another's lives. Then we light candles, pray an adapted form of the rosary, and listen to a reading from scripture and some recorded music suitable for meditation.

Simplicity is important. But the content of our prayer evening is solid. We pray for marriages and families, for one another, and for whatever concerns fill our hearts. Mostly, however, we support one another in our dedication to family lives of various kinds—even if it rarely surfaces in words. We support one another in our desire to be open to the Spirit of Christ precisely through our commitment to marriage and family life. And believe me, there is no prayer like the prayer of a group of parents for whom faith in Christ is the center of their lives and the goal of all they do.

Family prayers and rituals tend to be unique to each family. Each has its own style, its own traditions. The important thing is not so much *how* we pray and ritualize, as *that* we pray and ritualize. Linked with family times together and family ways of serving others, we find that family prayer and ritual strengthens our family in ways that nothing else can.

FAMILY FOCAL POINT 1

We are at a point in history, writes Sister Sandra DeGidio in her excellent book *Enriching Faith Through Family Celebrations,* when families are "developing a new level of appreciation and incorporation of ritual into their lives." This does not mean that families are merely rehashing old family devotions from the past, "but rather the creative development of new rituals for a new age to express the lived experiences of today, rituals that help us reflect on both our sacred and our secular experiences and see them as one."

Sister Sandra, who has spent much time with families and listening to families, writes that "nothing accomplishes family faith-sharing as effectively as ritual, which enables the family and community to express the faith within."

When children participate in family faith rituals, they grow to understand and appreciate their faith tradition in ways that no classroom program can communicate. They "become not just learners who have to know certain things in order to be Christian (as our religious education programs can often suggest), but sharers in the life and actions of the Christian community."

FAMILY FOCAL POINT 2

Today's family has a great hunger for ritual. Paradoxically, we see parents denying any such hunger. Why? Probably because they are uncomfortable with the idea of celebrating God openly and naturally with their children. What we see in this kind of family is that the children eventually seek ritual and prayer outside of the family or parish circle. . . .

How can the Catholic family replace the rituals and traditions lost since Vatican II with rituals meaningful to today's children? Most of today's families do not respond to rituals of an earlier age in our Church. . . . Most do respond to open prayer, song, and communal celebration. Our task as parents is to learn how to change, to adapt, to furnish new religious experiences in our homes so that our children will not have to seek them elsewhere.

—from *Family Prayer*, by Dolores Curran

Resources

Anzia, Joan, and Mary Durkin, *Marital Intimacy: A Catholic Perspective*. Loyola University Press, 1980.

Bender, Ross T., *Christians in Families*. Herald Press, 1982.

Briggs, Dorothy Corkille, *Your Child's Self-Esteem*. Doubleday, 1970.

Callahan, Sidney Cornelia, *Parenting: The Principles and Politics of Parenthood*. Doubleday, 1973.

Curran, Dolores, *Family Prayer*. St. Anthony Messenger Press, 1983.

——————, *Traits of a Healthy Family*. Winston Press, 1983.

DeGidio, Sr. Sandra, *Enriching Faith Through Family Celebrations*. Twenty-Third Publications, 1989.

John Paul II, *On The Family: Familiaris Consortio*. U.S. Catholic Conference, 1981.

Joy, Donald, *Parents, Kids and Sexual Integrity*. Word Books, 1988.

Lappe, Frances Moore and Family, *What to Do After You Turn Off the TV*. Ballantine Books, 1985.

Levitan, Sar A., et al., *What's Happening to the American Family?* Johns Hopkins University Press, 1988.

Pearce, Joseph Chilton, *Magical Child Matures*. Bantam Books, 1986.

Postman, Neil, *The Disappearance of Childhood*.

Delacorte Press, 1982.

Rubin, Jeffrey, and Carol Rubin, *When Families Fight.* Ballantine Books, 1990.

Thomas, John L., S.J., *Beginning Your Marriage.* ACTA Publications, 1987.